AF413437

RANDOM HOUSE
LARGE
PRINT

Praise for The Courage to Commit

"Shawn and Andrew are fire and light. And what I love most about them is that they didn't stop in the arena of sports. The same commitment that made them champions shows up in their families, their relationships, and the way they live out their calling. I trust them as coaches and guides. You won't be sorry you picked up this book!"

> —Jennie Allen, **New York Times** bestselling author of **Find Your People**

"**The Courage to Commit** has a message that needs to be shared with the world. Take it from these two superstars—commitment is key!"

> —Lewis Howes, **New York Times** bestselling author and host of **The School of Greatness**

"**The Courage to Commit** hits like a reminder that the real win is staying in the moment and building something from where you stand. It turns that restless grass-is-greener feeling into fuel to dig roots, stay, and create your own breakthrough right now."

> —Jordan Chiles, two-time Olympic gymnast and **New York Times** bestselling author

"In **The Courage to Commit**, Shawn Johnson and Andrew East show us how to stay in the game even when quitting feels easier. Read this practical, funny, and inspiring book to turn small commitments into lasting change."

> —Arthur C. Brooks, Harvard professor and #1 **New York Times** bestselling author

"Commitment is a bridge between who we are today and who we're being called to become. Our friends, Shawn and Andrew, understand that well. **The Courage to Commit** shows how saying yes to what matters most—over and over and over—can transform your marriage, your family, your faith, and your impact."

—Tim and Demi Tebow

"Shawn Johnson and Andrew East seem to have been handed the playbook for life at a young age. As a husband, father, business owner, and author, I'm thrilled they're sharing their secrets to living with unyielding commitment. Commit to reading this and then buckle up for what happens next!"

—Jon Acuff, **New York Times** bestselling author of **Soundtracks: The Surprising Solution to Overthinking**

"Shawn Johnson and Andrew East have written a desperately needed call to action for all of us who find ourselves anxious, burned-out, and grasping for avoidant hacks and workarounds. The freedom and joy we are all grinding and striving for is on the other side of worthy commitments, sustained effort and daily practices, and a willingness to persevere. In **The Courage to Commit**, Johnson and East show you how."

—Dr. John Delony, host of **The Dr. John Delony Show** and bestselling author

The Courage
to Commit

The Courage to Commit

EMBRACE THE RADICAL POWER
OF STICKING WITH SOMETHING

Shawn Johnson
and Andrew East

with Jimmy Soni

Published by Random House Large Print
in association with Portfolio/Penguin, an imprint of
Penguin Random House LLC, 1745 Broadway,
New York, NY 10019, penguinrandomhouse.com.

Original cover design: Brian Lemus
Design adapted for Large Print
Interior photos of Shawn Johnson and Andrew East
by Jessica Steddom. Used with permission.

The Library of Congress has established a
Cataloging-in-Publication record for this title.

FIRST LARGE PRINT EDITION

ISBN: 979-8-217-34932-6

Printed in the United States of America

1st Printing

The authorized representative in the EU for product safety
and compliance is Penguin Random House Ireland,
Morrison Chambers, 32 Nassau Street, Dublin D02 YH68,
Ireland, https://eu-contact.penguin.ie

CONTENTS

How

Introduction

Time stops when you're suspended in air.

In those weightless moments before a double-twisting double back—before gravity remembers you exist—there's a peculiar silence. The roar of thousands fades to white noise. Your heart, which moments ago hammered against your rib cage, seems to pause between beats. Twenty years of training, countless falls, torn calluses, and tearful nights compress into a single breath.

The move itself is a rebellion against physics: two complete rotations while simultaneously twisting twice, all in the span of a heartbeat. It's the kind of feat that makes physicists scratch their heads and gymnastics judges hold their breath.

As I stood on the beam at the 2008 Olympic Trials, chalk dust settling on my palms, I wasn't thinking about physics. I was thinking about the thousands of mornings I'd dragged myself to the gym when the world was still dark and silent. About the birthdays spent in physical therapy, the holidays watching competitions from the sidelines, nursing injuries. About all the times I'd fallen—literally and metaphorically—and somehow convinced myself to climb back up.

I didn't know then that this moment would become more than just a milestone in gymnastics. It would become a metaphor for everything my husband, Andrew, and I believe about life's most misunderstood force: commitment.

Commitment has an image problem.

In our swipe-right, job-hopping, "let's keep things casual" culture, it conjures balls and chains. Settling down as settling for less. Boring dinner conversations and beige suburban lawns stretching into eternity. Commitmentphobia has become a badge of honor.

Modern life seems designed to keep us uncommitted. Dating apps promise someone better is one swipe away. Career advice pushes us to job-hop every eighteen months. Even our entertainment comes with a skip button. We've built an entire economy around the fear of missing out, where keeping your options open passes for wisdom.

And yet here we are, two people who've made a

living off the power of doubling down. Olympic gold medals and NFL careers are forged in total commitment, where the only way out is through.

This book is our love letter to commitment in an age that treats it like a relic. But it's more than that. It's a manual.

Because here's what nobody tells you: Commitment is a skill. It has an infrastructure, a process, a set of practices that make it sustainable. Most advice on the subject boils down to "just stick with it"—as if dedication were simply a matter of gritting your teeth harder. That's like telling someone to "just be funnier" or "just run faster." It mistakes the outcome for the method.

We've learned—through years of elite athletics, marriage, entrepreneurship, and plenty of spectacular failures—that commitment has an architecture. There are ways to design your environment, your relationships, your daily rhythms so that staying the course becomes easier than giving up. There are practices that make recommitment feel natural rather than heroic. This book will show you what they are.

But first, we want to show you why it's worth it. Because commitment sparks adventure. It creates freedom through focus. When you go all in on something that matters, life gets richer, wilder, more electric. The commitment literature misses this— too busy preaching duty and discipline to notice that real commitment feels more like falling in love than forcing yourself to eat vegetables.

We're here to show you that version instead: the one that makes your life bigger, not smaller.

Let me tell you about my college football journey—a story that perfectly illustrates why most people get commitment completely wrong.

Picture this: an eighteen-year-old kid from Indianapolis who'd dreamed of playing Division I football, finally getting his shot at Vanderbilt. I was on an academic scholarship, balancing SEC football with a civil engineering degree. It should have been everything I'd worked for.

Instead, my freshman year was a disaster. I was failing three of my four classes—organic chemistry, multivariable calculus, and physics. Our team went 2 and 10. I got injured and wasn't contributing. I was doing what I thought was "trying hard," but nothing was working. I legitimately almost transferred. This was supposed to be my dream, but I was miserable and failing at what mattered most.

Then James Franklin arrived as our new head coach, and the entire program shifted—though not in a way any of us expected.

Franklin didn't just want to coach football. He wanted to transform us as human beings. No alcohol. Curfews. Four thirty a.m. workouts that made grown men vomit into trash cans scattered around the gym. Academic tutors. Mandatory study sessions. If you violated "training rules," you'd be doing 5 a.m. punishment workouts for a week while coaches patrolled to make sure you weren't partying.

Most of us hated it at first. This wasn't what we'd signed up for. We were college football players, not monks. But Franklin had something we didn't: a vision of what we could become if we committed completely, even when the outcome was unclear. His mantra was simple: Trust the process. Not just as a motivational slogan but as a way of life, one built on daily deposits of progress toward a larger commitment.

Here's what nobody talks about in those "find your passion" speeches: Sometimes the thing that changes your life looks nothing like what you thought you wanted. I could have transferred. I could have found an easier program, a more "fun" college experience. Instead, I made a choice that felt uncomfortable but somehow right: I decided to trust the process completely.

The results? I went from failing three classes to graduating early with two degrees—that engineering degree plus an MBA. Our team went from 2 and 10 to the most successful in Vanderbilt history. I became team captain for both my junior and senior years. But more importantly, I learned something that would shape every major decision in my life: When you stop looking for escape routes and commit fully to the hard thing in front of you, you discover reserves of capability you never knew existed.

This is nominally a story about football. Really, it's about what happens when you start treating your life like a craft.

Most commitment advice treats dedication like a character flaw you need to develop through sheer willpower. Work harder! Try more! Grit your teeth and bear it!

But that's not how commitment actually works. Real commitment is about creating an ecosystem that makes the right choices irresistible. It's about designing your life so that the path of least resistance leads toward the things that matter most.

Think of it like compound interest for your life choices. Every time you recommit to a person, a craft, or a cause, you're building momentum. You're stacking invisible gains, discovering depths and insights that only sustained attention reveals. At first, commitment can feel painfully boring, like nothing's happening. But those quiet, repeated efforts become unstoppable. We're wired to undervalue this—to miss how small actions, compounded over time, can radically reshape our lives. Stick with it, and the payoff is exponential.

We know what you might be thinking: "But what about spontaneity? What about keeping my options open? What about the very real possibility that I might choose wrong?"

These are fair questions. We live in the age of infinite scroll, where the next best thing is always just one click away. But here's a truth we had to learn the hard way: When you refuse to plant your feet firmly anywhere, you end up constantly second-guessing your choices, perpetually waiting for your "real" life to begin. You become a tourist in your own existence, sampling everything but savoring nothing. The truth is, every choice will fall short if you only ever dip your toes in. But when you go all in, even imperfect paths begin to reveal unexpected richness.

The uncommitted life can feel like freedom, but it's often just anxiety wearing a clever disguise.

Here's a truth that took us years to understand: The most meaningful moments in life don't announce themselves with fanfare. They're quiet decisions made time and time again out of the spotlight. For Andrew, it was showing up to the weight room two hours before practice, running drills alone on frost-covered fields while his teammates slept. For Shawn, it was returning to the gym the day after a crushing failure, hands still raw, pride still bruised, to try again.

These moments seem small in isolation. But string enough of them together, and they become the architecture of an extraordinary life. It's a principle that's shaped everything from our marriage to our careers, from how we parent to how we arrange our living room. (Yes, the living room. We'll explain.)

Commitment is a catalyst. It's what takes a scattered collection of interests and turns them into mastery, a series of dates into a marriage, a job into a calling. But—and here's where most self-help books go off the rails—not everything deserves your full commitment. Learning to choose wisely is just as important as learning to stick with your choices.

We'll show you the difference between commitments that energize you and those that merely deplete you. We'll give you tools to audit your current commitments and choose new ones that actually align with who you want to become.

Throughout this journey, we'll be honest about our failures too. Like the time Shawn nearly quit gymnastics after a devastating injury that seemed to mock twenty years of preparation. Or when Andrew's commitment to football wavered so dramatically that he became what coaches diplomatically call a "plan B guy." Or the countless small moments when Netflix won out over our business or family commitments.

What saved us wasn't some superhuman resolve. It

was learning to build systems that made recommitment easier than quitting—and learning to ask better questions when we felt like giving up. Questions like: Why does this matter? What am I actually committing to? And how do I keep showing up when the initial spark fades?

This book is our attempt to work through those questions—first for ourselves, and now with you. We've broken this journey into three parts, each centered on a question we've asked ourselves many times. We're not writing as experts, but as people who want to dig deeper—into our own stories, our patterns, and the wisdom of the coaches, mentors, and friends who've shaped how we think about commitment. Some of what we share comes from seasons where commitment enriched our lives in ways we didn't expect. Other times, it comes from moments when we backed away too soon—and learned the hard way what we were missing.

First, we'll explore the Why—and trust us, it goes deeper than you might think. We'll share groundbreaking research on how commitment literally rewires our brains, creating neural pathways that turn difficult choices into automatic habits. And you'll discover why the most successful people in any field often are the ones who simply stuck around long enough to compound their small advantages.

Next, we'll tackle the What—because not everything deserves your full commitment. We'll show you why seemingly small decisions about your environment can either drain or reinforce your commitment muscle. You'll learn how to distinguish between commitments that light you up and those that slowly burn you out.

Finally, we'll dive deep into the How—the nitty-gritty tactics and strategies that turn good intentions into lasting change. This is about designing your life in a way that makes commitment the default.

People often ask us what it feels like to achieve your dreams—to win Olympic gold, to play in the NFL, to build a life that once seemed impossible. The truth? Those peak moments are both more and less than you'd imagine. More, because they're proof of what humans can achieve through relentless commitment. Less, because they're just visible markers of a much deeper transformation that happens in the quiet moments, in the daily choices, in the predawn hours when no one is watching.

Remember that double-twisting double back we opened with? The actual moment of landing it lasted less than a second. But that second contained ten years of early mornings, over one hundred thousand repetitions of related skills, and thousands of small choices to stay committed when quitting would have been easier, more sensible, more **normal**.

That's why we wrote this book. Because we believe everyone has their own version of a double-twisting double back—their own impossible dream that feels just out of reach. Maybe it's starting a business that changes your industry. Maybe it's building a marriage that defies the statistics. Maybe it's transforming your health, your community, or your creative practice.

Whatever your version looks like, the path is the same: pick something that matters, and stay with it long enough to find out what it can become. Long enough for everyone else to move on to the next thing. Long enough to surprise yourself.

As you turn these pages, we invite you to think about your own relationship with commitment. What dreams have you deferred because they seemed too daunting? What goals have you abandoned because progress was too slow? What might be possible if you approached them with dedication to the process?

In a culture addicted to quick fixes and escape hatches, we've forgotten something essential: The most extraordinary lives are built on beautiful obsessions. On the willingness to say yes to one thing so completely that it transforms both what you can do and who you become. The age of infinite choice has given us everything except what we crave most: the exquisite freedom that comes from choosing.

So it's time to reclaim that freedom for ourselves. Time to stop scrolling and start building. Time to choose our obsessions as carefully as we choose our fears.

We've spent the past few years reverse-engineering the moments in our own lives that felt most alive, most aligned. What we found—across athletics, business, and family—was a common thread: The times we went all in were the times that shaped us most. And when we looked at the seasons where we felt restless or off track, we noticed something else: those were often the times we were hedging.

We're not here to preach. Maybe this just works for us. But we have a hunch it could work for you, too.

Let's go.

Why

Before diving into the what and how of commitment, we need to discuss the why. Because if you're anything like us, you've probably been conditioned to think of commitment as a bit of a drag—the responsible choice, the grown-up thing to do, the option that requires you to trade your Netflix password for a mortgage payment and call it progress.

We're here to tell you that story is false.

Over the next five chapters, we want to show you commitment's best-kept secrets: the rewards that nobody mentions in wedding speeches (probably because they're too busy talking about how marriage is "hard work") or commencement addresses (where they're focused on encouraging you to "follow your dreams" without explaining what happens when you actually catch one).

Calm might seem like an odd place to start, but it's commitment's most immediate gift. Choosing one path creates an almost shocking sense of peace in a world designed to scatter your attention across a thousand priorities. **Joy** follows close behind—the deeper satisfaction that comes from diving beneath life's surface rather than skimming across it. **Depth** transforms how you see everything, revealing hidden gems that others miss entirely.

Then things get really interesting. **Mastery** is about the peculiar magic that happens when skill becomes second nature, when you stop thinking about what you're doing and start dancing with it. And **Meaning**? Well, that's where commitment stops being just a personal choice and becomes a way of mattering in the world.

These are the actual treasures hiding behind what looks like limitation—rewards so rich that once you've tasted them, the old story about keeping your options open starts to feel a bit like choosing to stay hungry at a feast.

1

Calm

Imagine yourself standing in front of your closet on a Monday morning. The hangers hold a thoughtfully curated collection of clothes, each chosen for quality, fit, and purpose. There's no clutter, no dated impulse purchases, or "maybe someday" outfits. Just the essentials that serve you well. As you reach for your selected outfit, there's no paralysis or mental wrestling over what message each combination might convey. The decision is straightforward and almost effortless.

Now imagine another closet—one overflowing with options. Fast-fashion purchases vie with designer splurges. Trends from three seasons ago intertwine with "just in case" pieces that have never seen daylight. Each morning brings a new wave of decision fatigue as you wade through an overwhelming sea of choices.

Which closet brings you peace? The answer may seem obvious, yet we live in a culture that celebrates endless options, unlimited choices, and constant flexibility. But what if we have it wrong? What if the secret to a calmer, more centered life lies in the deliberate act of choosing—then letting go of the rest?

I still remember the exact moment I understood what commitment really meant. It was ten on a Friday night, and my phone buzzed with texts from friends heading to a party. I was lying on my couch, ice packs on both shoulders, watching film of my beam routine for the hundredth time that week.

"Come on, Shawn! Just for an hour!"

"You never come out anymore!"

"Live a little!"

Three years earlier, I would have agonized over this decision. Weighed the pros and cons. Told myself I deserved a break. Negotiated some compromise where I'd go "just for a bit" and definitely wouldn't drink and would absolutely be home by midnight.

But that Friday night? I texted "Have fun!" and went back to my film. No internal debate. No FOMO. No resentment. Just . . . peace.

Olympic training had transformed my world into something beautifully simple. Each day unfolded with the quiet rhythm of someone who knows exactly where they're going: 5 a.m. wake-up, stretch, breakfast, morning practice, recovery, lunch, afternoon training, dinner, film study, sleep. Repeat.

The grocery store became my favorite example of this transformation. I'd walk in and entire sections would blur beyond my peripheral vision like they were behind frosted glass. The snack aisle? Might as well have been selling car parts. The ice cream freezers? Just cold boxes holding nothing that concerned me. I wasn't fighting temptation—I had simply stepped into a different universe where those things didn't exist for me.

Friends thought I was living some kind of joyless, military-style existence. What they couldn't see was how this narrowing had actually expanded everything. Without the constant negotiations—Should I go out? What should I eat? How late can I stay up?—my mind was free. All that brainpower I used to spend on decisions now poured into my craft. Into perfecting that quarter turn on my dismount. Into finding an extra tenth of a point in my leap series.

The liberation was intoxicating. Every choice I didn't have to make was like dropping a heavy bag I didn't realize I'd been carrying.

This kind of peace might sound almost too simple to be profound. The modern self-help industry promises that the path to fulfillment runs through keeping every door open, every possibility alive. We're told to "follow our bliss," "keep our options open," and "never settle." Choice, we're assured, is power.

But what if this foundational assumption is wrong? What if the very thing we think will liberate us is the source of our restlessness?

The irony is that commitment—which our culture often frames as limitation—might be the secret ingredient to the calm we desperately seek. It's quieter than the flashy promises of self-optimization or the adrenaline rush of endless possibility. Calm doesn't sell books or generate clicks. It doesn't promise to transform your life in thirty days or unlock your hidden potential. It's subtler than that.

But for those who've experienced it, this particular gift of commitment feels revolutionary. When you eliminate the constant mental chatter of what-if scenarios and should-I-or-shouldn't-I deliberations, you open up brain space. Mental bandwidth that was once consumed by decision paralysis suddenly becomes available for deeper thinking, creative problem-solving, and simply being present in your life.

There's hard science behind why commitment creates calm. In 2011, researchers published a groundbreaking study on decision fatigue in **Proceedings of the National Academy of Sciences**. They found that judges were significantly more likely to grant parole to prisoners whose cases were heard early in the morning or right after a food break. As the judges made decision after decision, their mental energy diminished, causing them to default to the "safer" option of maintaining the status quo.

Every choice you make—whether it's what to wear, what to eat, or whether to respond to that after-hours email—draws on the same brainpower. When that well runs dry, we tend to make impulsive decisions or avoid making choices altogether. Both options lead to increased anxiety rather than peace.

This is commitment's quiet trick: Decide once what matters most, and a thousand smaller decisions disappear. It's like installing a powerful filter that screens out the nonessential, preserving your mental horsepower for what truly matters.

Consider President Obama's famously limited wardrobe during his presidency—only blue or gray suits. "I don't want to make decisions about what I'm eating or wearing," he told the author Michael Lewis. "Because I have too many other decisions to make." Mental energy is finite and must be consciously preserved. "You need to focus your decision-making energy," he reflected. "You need to routinize yourself. You can't be going through the day distracted by trivia."

The paradox is delightful: By seemingly limiting ourselves through commitment, we actually expand our capacity for peace and effectiveness.

 If Shawn's story illustrates the peace that comes from commitment, mine reveals the hidden cost of avoiding it—a low-grade anxiety that becomes so familiar you forget it's there until it's gone.

I was a top-rated long snapper coming out of college, with numerous teams expressing interest. On paper, I had everything lined up. But unlike in my Vanderbilt days, when football was the cornerstone of my identity, I found my focus scattered across a dozen possibilities.

The calls came in: the Patriots, the Chiefs, the Bears. Each conversation felt promising. But instead of choosing one path and committing fully, I kept my options open. I hedged my bets, cultivated backup plans, explored "just in case" scenarios. Looking back, I see it clearly: I was committed to football until I got cut for the first time. That shook something loose. I told myself I was being strategic. Really, I was protecting myself from the pain of another loss—if I never went all in, I could never be fully crushed. It felt wise. It diluted everything.

What I didn't realize was how exhausting it would become—and how visible. While I told teams that the NFL was my singular dream, I was simultaneously exploring venture capital opportunities and flirting with rugby. Coaches can spot a plan-B guy from a mile away. That's precisely what I had become: someone to potentially consider down the road rather than a must-have addition to their roster. There's a difference between being in the pros and being a pro, between occupying a roster spot and owning the responsibility that comes with it. One is about presence; the other is about posture, mindset, and daily habits. When you're competing against athletes who eat, sleep, and breathe football, even the slightest wavering becomes glaring.

The wake-up call came during my final NFL stint when a coach pulled me aside after watching film. "It doesn't look like you're trying here," he said, replaying a particular play. "Why is that?" The words hit like a physical blow. I had always been the effort guy. Yet here I was, being called out on the thing that had once defined me.

This pattern came to a head when I was signed to the (then) Washington Redskins. I'd just finished my first season when I got what felt like a once-in-a-lifetime opportunity: running the Boston Marathon. The catch? The race fell the day before I had to report for off-season training.

Football requires showing up heavy, focused on power and impact. Marathon running demands long runs and a lean physique. I convinced myself I could split the difference.

So I half-trained. I skipped the long runs because I needed to maintain 245 pounds of muscle mass. Did the shorter ones, told myself it would be enough. It wasn't.

My body locked up at mile sixteen. I needed two IVs to rehydrate, then rushed to the airport for training camp. The next morning, I limped into the team facility: underweight, dehydrated, and cramping through my physicals. I was showing up to my dream job in a partial, compromised state.

Here's the embarrassing part: This wasn't even the first time. In 2016, I went to a rugby tournament in Trinidad and Tobago during peak NFL tryout season. I was down there getting blisters and getting beat up when the New York Giants called—they needed a long snapper tomorrow. We found a red-eye, I stayed up all night trying to recover, and I bombed the tryout.

Twice I tried to diversify my opportunities. Twice I undermined my best one. Nine different teams cut me over those years, and I finally understood why.

That morning in the Redskins facility, sweating through a physical I wasn't prepared for, the lesson finally landed: Mastery demands full commitment.

Andrew's experience reveals a truth about the hidden mechanics of choice anxiety. What looked like rational decision-making from the outside—keeping doors open, building backup plans—was actually creating a feedback loop that amplified his stress while undermining his performance.

But why does this happen? Why does having more choices, which should theoretically give us more control, often leave us feeling less capable and more anxious?

The answer lies in understanding something important about how our brains process decisions. Recent research reveals that when we face an abundance of options, our bodies and minds enter a state of heightened engagement coupled with mounting stress, creating a perfect storm of caring more while feeling less capable.

In experiments at the University at Buffalo, researchers had people choose from either four or fifteen dating profiles while monitoring their heart rate and blood pressure. This allowed scientists to monitor two crucial psychological states: how much the decision mattered to participants and how capable they felt of making it well.

The results revealed a fascinating paradox. When faced with many options rather than few, people's bodies showed simultaneous signs of both heightened investment and increased threat. Their cardiovascular patterns revealed they were more engaged—their hearts pumped harder and faster, indicating they saw the choice as deeply meaningful. Yet their blood-flow patterns simultaneously showed classic signs of feeling overwhelmed and incapable.

But here's what makes this research particularly illuminating: This wasn't about just the moment of choice. The physiological stress actually intensified as participants moved from browsing to deciding, suggesting that having more options doesn't only make the initial evaluation harder—it makes the final commitment feel more fraught.

Think about Andrew's experience through this lens. Each new team that called didn't just add another option—it amplified the stakes of every decision he made. Should he take that venture capital meeting? The choice felt weightier precisely because he had so many other possibilities in play. Should he commit fully to one team's tryout when another team teased interest? The decision became paralyzing because saying yes to one thing meant potentially saying no to everything else.

This explains why choice abundance creates such a specific kind of suffering. You're dealing with the psychological burden of each choice mattering more while simultaneously feeling less equipped to choose wisely. It's like being asked to make the most important decision of your life while someone is shaking the table.

The research helps explain why commitment brings such profound relief. When we commit deeply to something—whether it's a career path or a relationship—we transform decision-making itself. Our intense engagement becomes an asset rather than a source of paralysis because we've aligned what matters deeply to us with what we're actually capable of managing well.

In Shawn's training environment, the question was never whether the workout mattered—of course it did. But equally important, she never had to question her ability to make the right choice about showing up, because the framework of commitment had already made that choice for her. The path was clear, and clarity breeds calm.

Commitment's greatest gift is calm—the deep, abiding peace that comes when you stop carrying the weight of infinite possibility and start enjoying the lightness of chosen direction.

This might feel like a strange place to end our exploration of calm, but it's actually where the real work begins. Because if you're anything like us, you're probably thinking: "Okay, I'm sold on the idea that commitment creates calm. But commit to what, exactly? How do I know I'm choosing the right thing? What if I pick wrong and waste years of my life?"

These are the right questions, and the later parts of the book will help you answer them. We'll explore how to identify what deserves your deepest dedication, how to distinguish between worthy commitments and mere distractions, and how to build the kind of sustainable devotion that enriches rather than depletes your life.

But for now, we want you to sit with this foundational truth: Real freedom might come from the revolutionary act of closing some doors. Not all of them—just enough to let you walk confidently through the ones that matter.

Think of this as permission to stop auditioning for every possible version of your life. You can let some alternate futures go. You can choose to stop being interested in certain opportunities. You can allow entire aisles of possibility to fade from your mental landscape, because you're finally free to focus on what you've chosen to care about most.

The grocery store gets smaller. Somehow, your life gets larger. That's calm's quiet promise: that in choosing less, you might just find more. And in a world that seems designed to scatter our attention across a thousand different urgencies, that promise feels like a refuge worth seeking.

EVERY CHOICE COSTS SOMETHING. Each decision draws from the same finite reserves. When that well runs dry, anxiety rises and judgment falters.

MORE OPTIONS MAKE CHOOSING HARDER. Abundance triggers a paradox: We care more about getting it right while feeling less capable of doing so.

BACKUP PLANS BROADCAST DOUBT. Keeping alternatives alive divides attention, signals uncertainty to others, and creates a quiet hum of anxiety about whether you're on the right path.

COMMITMENT WORKS LIKE A FILTER. Deep dedication to what matters screens out the nonessential. Whole categories of decisions simply disappear.

CLARITY CREATES CALM. When you've already decided what you're doing, you stop carrying the weight of infinite possibility. The path forward becomes obvious.

2

Joy

The kip almost broke me.

It's a foundational gymnastics skill—the kind that looks simple and makes beginners cry. For a year, I practiced it, failing hundreds, maybe thousands of times. Each attempt left me more frustrated than the last. My hands were raw; my confidence was shot. The kip kept me up at night, replaying the motion in my mind, analyzing what had gone wrong. It made me question everything: my talent, my future, whether I was cut out for this sport at all.

Coaches will tell you: The kip is where many gymnasts' dreams end. It's the great filter, the skill that separates those who will continue from those who will find other passions.

What nobody mentions is that surviving the filter comes with its own reward. The day I finally landed that kip—a basic move, invisible on any scorecard—I felt something that rivaled any Olympic podium I would later stand on.

The feeling was so pure, so complete, that I remember exactly where I was standing, what the gym smelled like, even the expression on my coach's face. "If you can learn this skill," he told me that day, "you can learn anything in the sport."

He was right, but not in the way he meant. What I learned about was the peculiar alchemy that happens when you commit completely to something: how the very act of choosing one path fully—even if it's hard, even if it seems impossible, even if no one else understands why it matters so much—can unlock a kind of joy that casual pursuits never touch.

And the most extraordinary part? That joy isn't reserved for the elite or the exceptional. It's available to all of us—because it comes not from talent or luck, but from simply choosing a different mindset.

That moment with the kip speaks to something about commitment that our culture has gotten spectacularly wrong: We've been told a story that frames dedication as the enemy of delight—as if choosing one path means resigning ourselves to a life of grim determination and joyless duty. In our collective imagination, commitment has become synonymous with settling, sacrificing, and giving up the good stuff for the responsible stuff.

When we were on tour recently, someone in the audience posed a question that perfectly captured this cultural assumption: "You two live such structured lives—how do you make space for joy?" The implication was unmistakable: Surely all this planning and commitment must somehow crowd out spontaneity and wonder.

We understand why people think this way. We've been conditioned to believe that joy happens to us—a lucky accident, a chance encounter, a moment of serendipity. Our culture particularly loves the myth of spontaneous joy: the unplanned adventure, the whimsical decision, the path not taken. We're told that having endless choices is the surest route to happiness, that commitment is where dreaming stops.

It's a seductive story. It's also completely wrong.

What we want to show you in this chapter is that the deepest, most lasting joys come from walking fully through the doors we choose. The richest joys are cultivated through focus and care. Far from being joy's opposite, commitment might be its secret ingredient.

Our cultural narratives glorify the early days of romance: the butterflies, the uncertainty, the intoxicating rush of possibility. Dating apps promise endless options, and romantic comedies usually end at the wedding. The implicit message is clear: Commitment is where excitement goes to die.

But ask any couple who's been together for decades and they'll tell you something that might surprise you: The deepest joys often come after the commitment, not before. Research backs this up in fascinating ways. Studies have found that couples with stable, high relationship satisfaction report significantly more positive affect and well-being than those in newer relationships—not despite their commitments, but because of them.

"I wish I could get married to him today," Shawn says of our relationship after ten years, "because I had no idea what love truly was back then." It's not that the wedding day wasn't joyful—it was. But the private languages that develop over time, the way we can communicate across a crowded room with just a glance, the shared history that changes the mundane into the meaningful—these are treasures that only commitment can unlock.

The research reveals why this happens. When you're dating someone new, you might spend 30 percent of your brain cells wondering if they like your texts, if you're being too forward, if that joke landed wrong. But in a committed relationship, all that mental bandwidth gets freed up for something else: the creation of shared joy. Those silly dances in the kitchen while doing dishes. The inside jokes that make no sense to anyone else. The comfortable silences that feel like home.

Commitment acts like a greenhouse for joy—a protected space where delight can actually take root. The security of commitment creates the psychological safety needed for playfulness, vulnerability, and spontaneity to flourish. When you know someone will still love you tomorrow, you're more likely to start an impromptu pillow fight today. When you're not worried about maintaining a perfect image, you can let yourself be silly, imperfect, real.

This pattern repeats across every domain where humans find deep satisfaction. The musician who commits to daily practice discovers subtle beauties in the music that casual listeners never hear. The writer who shows up at the desk every morning, even when inspiration feels distant, experiences the unique thrill of watching rough ideas transform into polished prose—a joy invisible to the outside world but electric to those who've earned it through persistence.

When you commit fully to something—whether it's a relationship, a craft, or a calling—you develop what psychologists call "perceptual expertise." Like a sommelier who can detect notes in wine that others miss, or a bird-watcher who can distinguish dozens of species by their calls, committed attention reveals layers of richness that were always there, waiting to be discovered by someone willing to look deeply enough.

The researchers found that long-term couples were more likely to engage in what they call "shared meaning-making"—turning even mundane moments into opportunities for connection and joy. A trip to the grocery store becomes an adventure. A minor mishap becomes tomorrow's funny story. The security of commitment allows couples to find gold in the ordinary moments that newer relationships might miss entirely.

This has profound implications beyond just romantic relationships. It suggests that commitment itself might be a crucial ingredient in cultivating lasting joy—because it creates the conditions under which joy can deepen and expand. Like a tree that needs deep roots to grow tall, perhaps our capacity for joy needs the anchoring of commitment to reach its full height.

Commitment's ability to generate joy extends further than romantic relationships. Consider people with social anxiety—individuals who typically approach life with hesitation and restraint. Researchers studying this group discovered that when these individuals fully committed to pursuing their deepest purpose on a given day, they experienced dramatically higher levels of happiness, even amid challenges that would normally paralyze them with stress.

For example, one participant described committing to lead a community workshop despite intense anxiety. The anxiety didn't disappear, but it became background noise to a larger symphony of purpose and engagement. What would have been torture became, if not easy, at least meaningful and even joyful in unexpected moments.

Think about that for a moment. The very act of going all in, of saying "this matters enough to try," transformed their entire emotional landscape.

We see this constantly. When Andrew first started our YouTube channel, he approached it tentatively, treating it like a casual experiment. "I'll try this for a while," he said, "see how it goes." The videos were fine, but they felt flat, dutiful. After all, he'd once gone all in on football, poured everything into that dream, only to watch it unravel in ways that still hurt. Experimenting was safer. It was a way to stay protected. Underneath was a quiet fear: **What if I give my all again, and it still doesn't work out?** But then, one day, something shifted. He made the decision to commit fully—not just to making content, but to telling authentic stories that might actually change lives.

The transformation was immediate and profound. Suddenly, he started enjoying: the creative challenge of finding the perfect shot, the thrill of capturing a genuine moment, even the satisfaction of solving technical problems that would have been pure frustration before. What once were tedious details became entertaining puzzles. What was once anxiety about audience reception became excitement about connection.

The work itself hadn't changed, and the challenges hadn't disappeared. But his commitment had transformed those obstacles into sources of unexpected pleasure. This is what commitment does: It turns obstacles into puzzles you actually want to solve. The chef comes to love the methodical prep work that once felt like drudgery. The runner discovers pleasure in sensations that once signaled only pain. The parent finds meaning in the mundane moments of caregiving that once felt like pure sacrifice.

And here's what's remarkable: This creates a self-reinforcing cycle. The deeper we commit, the more sources of joy we discover, which makes us want to commit even more deeply. It's the opposite of the fear-based hesitation that keeps us sampling life's surface. Commitment expands our capacity for joy in ways we could never have imagined from the outside.

Every Sunday, we practice what we call "day of delight"—a commitment, paradoxically, to joy itself. We keep actual lists of activities that bring us delight, and on Sundays we do the things on the list and nothing else. No checking email, no spontaneous errands, no guilt about productivity. Some might see this as overly structured, maybe even rigid, but we've discovered that what used to be a day shadowed by anxiety—the slow creep of the "Sunday scaries"—has become our favorite day of the week.

The "nothing else" part turns out to be crucial. It's not enough to plan joyful activities if you're still mentally available to everything else competing for your attention. By creating firm boundaries—this time is sacred, these activities matter, everything else can wait—we've learned to be genuinely present in a way that feels almost revolutionary in our distracted age.

Why does this work so powerfully? Because when you've committed to something—really committed—you're free from the constant low-grade anxiety of wondering if you should be doing something else. You're no longer half present, one eye on your phone, one part of your mind cycling through your to-do list. You can be fully there, completely immersed in the moment, whether that's building a fort with the kids or taking an afternoon nap without guilt.

This is what researchers call "attention residue"—the mental energy we waste when we're constantly switching between tasks or questioning our choices. Commitment eliminates this waste. When you know Sunday is for passion, when you've already decided that this time is sacred and these activities matter, you can pour yourself fully into the experience.

By being more structured about joy, we've become more spontaneous within that structure. Knowing that we're committed to this time means we can let ourselves be silly, playful, completely absorbed.

This brings us to a deeper question: If commitment reliably creates conditions for joy, why does our culture resist this truth so fiercely? Why do we keep chasing the myth that more options, flexibility, and open doors will somehow lead to greater happiness?

The answer lies in understanding something important about how our brains process satisfaction itself. We've been focusing on how commitment adjusts our experience of the things we choose, but there's an equally important story about how commitment affects our relationship to the act of choosing.

The science behind this is fascinating and challenges some of our most basic assumptions about what makes us happy. In a landmark 2000 study, researchers Sheena Iyengar and Mark Lepper discovered that people who faced fewer choices didn't just make decisions more easily but felt more satisfied afterward. When presented with a limited array of options (six varieties of jam versus twenty-four, or a handful of essay topics versus thirty), participants chose more confidently and derived greater pleasure from their selections.

This finding turns our cultural logic on its head. We assume that more options equal more joy, that having endless possibilities is the royal road to satisfaction. However, the research suggests the opposite: Having too many choices can lead to what psychologists call "choice overload"—a state of decision paralysis that diminishes our capacity for enjoyment.

But the relationship between commitment and joy goes deeper than just avoiding decision fatigue. It's about fundamentally changing the quality of the satisfaction we derive from our choices. Studies in positive psychology have found that people who make and stick to meaningful commitments report higher levels of what researchers call "eudaimonic well-being"—the kind of deep, sustained happiness that comes from living a life of purpose and engagement.

This pattern holds even in professional contexts. Research has shown that experts who deeply commit to their fields experience more frequent states of "flow," that coveted mental state where joy and performance peak simultaneously. Musicians who practice with focus and intensity show distinct neural patterns during flow states that less experienced musicians don't exhibit, suggesting that sustained commitment literally rewires the brain for optimal creative experiences.

These studies reveal that commitment changes

both what we experience and how deeply we can experience it. Sustained dedication literally reshapes our neurological capacity for satisfaction.

When I work with young gymnasts today, I see this research play out in the most beautiful, tangible ways. These kids arrive at the gym with the same cultural programming we all carry: that joy should feel easy, that struggle signals you're on the wrong path, that commitment means giving up fun for grim determination.

Then they—like the younger me!—encounter the kip.

At first, they see only the frustration, the difficulty, the endless repetition. Their parents often ask me the same question we heard on tour: "How do we keep this fun for them?" The assumption is always that the commitment—showing up day after day, the willingness to fail repeatedly—will somehow drain the joy away.

But those who stick with it discover beauty in the struggle itself. They develop what I can only call "educated joy"—the deep satisfaction that comes from understanding something intimately enough to appreciate its subtleties.

"This was my hardest skill ever," I tell them when they're in the thick of it, and I watch their eyes light up with recognition. They realize they're part of a lineage, that every gymnast who came before them wrestled with this impossible movement. In that moment, they're learning something that will serve them outside the gym: that commitment can be a source of joy, that difficulty and delight aren't opposites but dance partners.

The transformation is remarkable to witness. A skill that once brought only tears becomes a source of pride. But more than that, these young athletes approach other challenges differently. They've discovered that landing the skill is one reward. Becoming someone who doesn't quit is the bigger one.

This is commitment's ultimate gift: It changes the very texture of our joy. Instead of the shallow pleasure of easy wins, we develop a capacity for the happiness that comes from knowing you've paid the full price for something precious. It's the difference between finding a $20 bill on the sidewalk and saving for months to buy something you really want. Both might make you happy, but only one makes you proud.

Years later, when these gymnasts face other challenges—in school, in relationships, in careers—they carry with them this secret knowledge: that the sweetest joys are often hidden inside the hardest work, waiting to be discovered by those brave enough to commit fully to the process.

JOY LIVES ON THE FAR SIDE OF DIFFICULTY. The kip, a basic gymnastics move, took a year to learn. Landing it produced a euphoria that rivaled Olympic ceremonies. The hardest skills yield the deepest satisfactions.

SECURITY UNLOCKS SPONTANEITY. Long-term couples experience more daily joy than new relationships. When you're not performing or auditioning, you can be silly, imperfect, real.

COMMITMENT REVEALS HIDDEN LAYERS. Like a sommelier detecting notes others miss, sustained attention develops perceptual expertise. The world becomes richer to those who look closely.

STRUCTURE PROTECTS DELIGHT. Boundaries create sacred space where happiness can flourish. "Day of delight" works because it excludes everything else.

THE JUICE IS IN THE JOURNEY. Mastering something changes the nature of satisfaction itself. You develop a capacity for happiness that scattered attention never builds.

3

Depth

People often ask me how I got into beekeeping. They expect a story about environmental activism or maybe a honey-based business venture. Instead, I tell them about moonshine.

My great-grandfather Madison Odell needed his apple trees pollinated for his distilling operation. The bees were a practical solution to a practical problem. But what started as a straightforward transaction between man and nature became something far more profound, stretching across four generations of my family.

The last words my grandfather spoke to my father were "take care of the bees." It was the passing of a torch, the transfer of a commitment that had already transformed from necessity into devotion.

My dad took that charge seriously, but in his

unique way. Where most beekeepers stick to the basics—simple sugar water for feeding—he became a kind of mad scientist of bee nutrition. He'd concoct these elaborate mixtures, convinced he could help our colonies thrive through whatever challenges they faced. I used to tease him about being an overprotective bee parent. Still, his experimental approach revealed something crucial about commitment: When you go all in on something, you start seeing possibilities others miss.

I inherited this legacy somewhat reluctantly. At first, it felt more like an obligation than a calling. But something interesting happened as I stayed with it: The world of bees slowly revealed itself in layers, each one more fascinating than the last.

I discovered that bees have their own language—a sophisticated dance-based communication system that shames our most advanced algorithms. I learned to read the subtle changes in their behavior that signal weather shifts days before any forecast. I began to understand how a single hive operates as both a superorganism and a collection of individuals, each with its role in the whole.

When Shawn and I started dating, I couldn't wait to share this world with her. So on our second date, I took her to the hives. This was not my smoothest move: Bees, it turned out, were her greatest fear. And in my enthusiasm, I might have overlooked some basic safety protocols. Like providing a proper bee suit.

The resulting sting could have ended our

beekeeping adventures and budding romance. But something unexpected happened at that moment when she was facing her fears. Even through the pain and panic, my excitement and passion revealed to her a snapshot of what had captured four generations of my family's imagination.

This is what commitment—even to bees!—does. It turns the mundane into the meaningful, the ordinary into the extraordinary. Bees are a common feature of everyday life, often overlooked and forgotten by passersby. But by choosing depth over breadth, we discover entire universes within what others might dismiss as unremarkable or straightforward. The bees taught me that. And they're still teaching me, one generation at a time.

What happened to Andrew's family across four generations of beekeeping illustrates what science is only beginning to understand. His great-grandfather saw bees as a practical necessity. His grandfather developed an emotional attachment. His father became a kind of bee whisperer, able to diagnose problems and predict behaviors that baffled other keepers. Each generation developed different ways of seeing and understanding these creatures.

This transformation is neurological. When Andrew's father worked with the bees, he drew on what researchers call "cognitive adaptation"—the literal rewiring of neural pathways that happens when we commit deeply to sustained, focused engagement with something complex.

Take Andrew's father's ability to read a hive's health with just a glance. What looks like a chaotic swarm of insects to most people appeared to him as an intricate ballet of signals and patterns. He noticed the angle of returning foragers' flights, the subtle changes in the guard bees' posture, the barely perceptible shift in the hive's collective hum. This is a fundamentally different way of processing sensory information, developed through decades of committed attention.

Anders Ericsson's landmark research on expertise development revolutionized how we think about mastery. He discovered that this kind of transformation requires more than just time. It demands what he calls "deliberate practice," focused and intentional engagement that pushes us beyond our comfort zones. The casual observer accumulates facts; the committed practitioner develops new forms of perception.

A fascinating 2025 study in **Brain Mechanisms** illustrated this perfectly by studying chess grandmasters. When these experts look at a board, they're not just drawing on memorized strategies or calculating possible moves. Brain scans revealed that their visual processing patterns have evolved to be different from those of novices. They see relationships and possibilities that others miss entirely because their brains have been sculpted by commitment to perceive the game in ways that casual players never will.

Whether you're a musician who can "feel" a piece's emotional architecture, a programmer who sees elegant solutions in seemingly chaotic code, or a parent who can distinguish between five different types of baby cries in the middle of the night, deep commitment creates what philosopher Maurice Merleau-Ponty called "embodied knowledge"—understanding that becomes so fundamental it feels like an extension of your senses.

Consider cycling—something particularly close to our family's heart. (Andrew's dad had him and his brothers racing in national competitions by age eleven; one brother became a world-class cyclist, and our son Jett learned to ride at just eighteen months old.) Merleau-Ponty used bicycle riding to illustrate how real knowledge works: You can't learn to ride by reading manuals or watching videos. The knowledge lives not in your conscious mind but in your body—in the thousands of tiny adjustments you make to maintain balance, your intuitive sense of how speed affects stability, and the way your body learns to lean into turns.

Try to explain how you ride a bike, and you'll quickly realize the impossibility of fully articulating this knowledge. Your body knows it, even if your mind can't quite explain it. This is the kind of knowing that deep commitment creates—a wisdom that transcends conscious thought.

Just as a skilled carpenter can "feel" when wood is ready to split, or an experienced chef can sense exactly when to flip a pancake without setting a timer, sustained engagement creates a melding of doer and doing, where the boundary between self and skill begins to blur.

By narrowing our focus, we expand our understanding. Commitment teaches us new ways of seeing.

This neurological rewiring that Andrew's father experienced with bees represents just one dimension of how commitment changes your perception. But there's another, perhaps even more profound way that depth changes us—not just how we see the world, but how we move through it.

I've lived this transformation in the most literal way possible: flying through the air. When people watch Olympic gymnastics, they see four minutes of apparent perfection—graceful lines, gravity-defying flips, and stick-the-landing precision. What they don't see is how a decade of daily face-plants fundamentally altered my relationship with the impossible.

Those thousands of hours in the gym created something far more valuable than muscle memory—they built embodied courage. Each failed attempt at a double-twisting double back (and there were hundreds) was rewiring my fundamental understanding of what constitutes reasonable risk versus reckless abandon.

Think about what it means to commit to throwing yourself fifteen feet into the air to rotate 720 degrees before landing on your feet. By any rational measure, this is insane. Yet through sustained commitment, my body learned to distinguish between "dangerous" and "merely terrifying." You can't think through a double twist at 400 rotations per minute—by the time your brain processes what's happening, you're already face down in the foam.

Instead, you develop "intelligent fearlessness"— the ability to work with danger rather than just push through it. Your nervous system learns to calculate complex equations of motion and momentum without consulting your conscious mind, distinguishing between the kind of fear that protects you and the kind that limits you.

But here's what I find most fascinating about this depth: It fundamentally alters your relationship with uncertainty itself. Once your body has learned to navigate the space between "impossible" and "inevitable" thousands of times, you develop an almost philosophical understanding of mastery. You realize that the goal isn't to eliminate risk or fear, but to develop such intimate knowledge of both that you can dance with them gracefully.

This shifts how you approach everything else in life. In business negotiations, I can sense the difference between productive tension and destructive conflict. In parenting, I've learned to distinguish between the challenges that help children grow and those that overwhelm them. The depth I developed in gymnastics taught me something: There's always a narrow pathway between "too safe" and "too dangerous." Finding it requires embodied wisdom, the kind that only comes from sustained commitment to navigating uncertainty.

These days, instead of foam pits, my learning happens in boardrooms and nurseries. The falls might be metaphorical, but the process of building depth is the same: Try, adjust, repeat, until what once seemed unthinkable becomes not just possible, but natural.

What Shawn discovered through gymnastics—that depth fundamentally changes our relationship with uncertainty—points to something even more remarkable about commitment's transformative power. The changes don't stay contained within our chosen domain. They ripple outward, enhancing our capabilities in ways that seem almost magical.

This phenomenon has fascinated researchers for decades. They call it "far transfer"—the way expertise in one domain enhances capabilities in seemingly unrelated areas. A fascinating body of research has shown that musicians tend to be particularly skilled at pattern recognition, even in non-musical contexts. Studies have found that long-term musical training influences functional connectivity between motor and multisensory brain areas, creating networks that are better trained to act jointly. The deep engagement required to master an instrument develops cognitive frameworks that prove useful across many domains.

That said, it's important to distinguish far transfer from the Dunning-Kruger effect—the cognitive bias where people who are highly competent in one field assume their expertise automatically carries over into others. Mastering Mozart doesn't mean you'll be a natural at macroeconomics, political forecasting, or predicting viral TikTok trends. But what deep mastery can offer is a sharpened set of mental tools—attentional control, pattern recognition, and resilience—that can support learning and problem-solving across new, unfamiliar territory.

This effect shows up everywhere once you start looking for it. Children who deeply engage with a second language often display enhanced problem-solving abilities in mathematics. Expert chess players frequently excel at strategic thinking in business. The transfer happens because deep commitment develops cognitive flexibility—the mental agility to see connections and possibilities that others might miss.

Think of it like tuning an instrument: When you carefully calibrate one string, it becomes easier to bring the others into harmony. When you develop depth in one area, you're not just becoming better at that specific skill—you're training your brain to perceive patterns, navigate complexity, and think systematically in ways that enhance everything else you do.

We've experienced this kind of resonance through-out our journey together, watching how the discipline we cultivated as athletes gave us tools that proved invaluable in business and family life. Learning to see in the dark provides a perfect metaphor: Once your eyes adjust to deeper levels of perception in one area, that enhanced vision tends to illuminate other parts of your life as well.

This spillover became especially clear to me during one of the more humbling chapters of my athletic career. When I was struggling with performance anxiety—the dreaded yips—during my NFL stint, I tried everything: sports psychologists, meditation apps, probably even a lucky charm or two.

What ultimately saved me was the most basic thing imaginable: trusting my body and the thou-sands of repetitions I had already completed, and telling my overthinking brain to please, for the love of all that's holy, just get out of the way. Once I stopped second-guessing every motion and let my muscle memory take over, the precision returned. The snaps became automatic again, flying true to their target without conscious thought—just as they had thousands of times in practice.

All those years of studying defensive and special teams formations—hours spent memorizing patterns that would make a chess master weep—had given me something unexpected. When we started analyzing market trends for our business ventures, I spotted patterns with the same intuitive recognition I'd developed for reading opposing teams. Who knew that understanding how a safety might cheat toward the strong side would help me predict consumer behavior?

Even more surprising was how our family's bee-keeping tradition became an unexpected guide to social situations. Four generations of learning to read subtle shifts in bee behavior—the way foragers adjust their flight patterns before weather changes, or how nurse bees cluster tighter around the queen under stress—had turned me into some kind of human emotion detector. I could pick up on microexpressions in business negotiations, sense when Shawn was processing something difficult even before she said a word, or recognize when our kids were about to have a meltdown in Target. (Though I should note that understanding these situations and responding appropriately are still two very different skill sets. I suspect I'm much better at the first than the second.)

When you've spent years breaking down complex physical movements into manageable chunks, creating family schedules becomes surprisingly manageable. When you've learned to maintain focus through endless repetitive drills, staying present during the seventeenth viewing of Frozen feels almost meditative. Almost.

The ability to maintain perspective through setbacks, trust in the long-term process over short-term results, and break down seemingly impossible challenges into achievable steps became my universal life tools. They are equally useful for fourth-and-short situations and figuring out how to get three kids ready for school without anyone crying. (Results may vary on that last one.)

The world seems engineered to keep us skimming: another notification, another tab, another fleeting dopamine hit of something new. There's something oddly countercultural about saying, "This. This is what I'm going to pour myself into." Like the choice to read a novel in a world of headlines, or learning to cook in an age of meal-delivery apps.

We see this tension constantly in our media business. YouTube's algorithms reward variety, constant content, the steady stream of new and trending topics. Yet our most meaningful work—the content that actually changes lives—comes from going deep. Really understanding our audience. Crafting stories with care. Building relationships that last years, not just until the next video drops. Nine years and thousands of videos later, with over seven billion views, our audience tells us that this content is making a difference in their lives, even as the platform's preferred trends shift around us.

We often joke about how our commitment to depth makes us seem almost old-fashioned. While friends hop between projects and pursuits like they're channel surfing, we've chosen to sink roots. Whether it's our marriage, our business, or yes, even our bees, we've discovered that the most extraordinary experiences often hide behind what looks like ordinary dedication.

This is what depth ultimately offers: not just expertise, but an entirely new way of seeing. We've experienced this transformation ourselves, watching it ripple through every area in which we've chosen to go deep. The same bee colony that once looked like chaos now appears as an intricate dance of signals and purpose. What once seemed like "just flips and twists" in gymnastics revealed itself as a sophisticated language of momentum and force, each movement carrying its own physics lesson.

Commitment gives you new eyes, allowing you to perceive layers of reality that were always there but remained invisible to casual observation. This enhanced perception comes with a trade-off. You won't be the person who's sampled every new work-out trend or mastered the latest productivity hack. But what you gain is something far more valuable: the ability to see beneath the surface of things, to perceive what others miss entirely.

It's like trading a thousand glimpses for one long look—and discovering that the longer you look, the more there is to see.

COMMITMENT REWIRES YOUR BRAIN. Chess grandmasters see boards differently than novices. Their visual processing has evolved through practice. Expertise changes perception at the neurological level.

MASTERY LIVES IN THE BODY. You can't learn to ride a bike from a manual. Deep knowledge becomes embodied wisdom, a kind of understanding that transcends conscious thought.

DEPTH SPILLS OVER. Reading football formations sharpens pattern recognition for market trends. Understanding bee behavior attunes you to human microexpressions. Expertise in one domain illuminates others.

REPETITION BUILDS INTELLIGENT FEARLESSNESS. Thousands of attempts teach you to distinguish between "dangerous" and "merely terrifying." You learn to dance with uncertainty.

ORDINARY THINGS CONTAIN UNIVERSES. Bees look like chaos to most people. To a fourth-generation beekeeper, they're an intricate ballet of signals. Commitment makes the flat multidimensional.

CHOOSING DEPTH IS COUNTERCULTURAL. In an age of infinite feeds and constant novelty, saying "This is what I'm pouring myself into" becomes a quiet rebellion.

4

Mastery

The first time I tried to do a forward roll, my mom says I cried. Not the gentle tears of a scraped knee, but the full-body sobs of a three-year-old whose world has momentarily collapsed. The gym mat—which to my tiny body offered barely any cushion between me and the hard floor—felt like an endless expanse of blue stretching out before me. My tiny hands pressed against its surface, testing its give. The instructor kept saying it was simple: Tuck your chin, roll forward. But my body wouldn't listen. It was as if someone had asked me to rearrange the solar system.

I tell this story not because it's particularly special—any parent who's watched their child learn to walk or ride a bike knows this moment of paralysis before a new skill. I tell it because thirteen years later, when I stood before thousands at the Olympics preparing to attempt one of the most difficult moves in gymnastics history, that same blue mat stretched out before me. Only this time, my hands knew exactly what to do. The double-twisting double back had become as natural to me as walking.

The distance between those two moments—the terrified toddler and the Olympic athlete—isn't marked in years or miles but in repetitions. People often ask me how many times I practiced that Olympic routine. It's the wrong question. The right question is how many forward rolls I did before they became boring. How many cartwheels before they felt like breathing. How many basic jumps before my body understood, on a cellular level, what it meant to leave the ground and return to it safely.

I've done the math: over one hundred thousand repetitions of fundamental skills. That's not counting the times I practiced in my mind while eating breakfast, or the ghost routines I performed in my bedroom at night, or the countless times I watched videos of other gymnasts, my muscles twitching in sympathetic motion.

Outsiders look at someone at the peak of their craft and think: magic. But it's just time. It's just commitment. One person has simply been doing the work longer. Mastery hides in the boring parts, and over time, the boring becomes beautiful.

Mastery is a relationship you build with a skill

over time. Like any long-term relationship, it has its moments of frustration, of wanting to quit, of wondering if it's all worth it. But also like any good bond, these challenges deepen rather than diminish the connection. It becomes an obsession, but the healthiest kind, one that feeds your soul rather than consuming it.

The secret that every elite athlete knows but rarely speaks about is that mastery isn't really about the final performance. The gold medal moment—what the crowd sees—is just the visible tip of an iceberg built from thousands of smaller, private victories. The first time you stick a landing without your coach's hand on your back. The day you finally understand how to engage your core in exactly the right way. These moments, invisible to everyone else, are where mastery actually lives.

There's nothing particularly revolutionary about saying that commitment leads to mastery. It's like noting that water is wet, or that practice makes perfect, or that assembling IKEA furniture will test your marriage.

And yet, like many fundamental truths, its very obviousness masks its profound importance. The fact that every human culture has developed some version of "practice makes perfect" isn't evidence of the idea's banality—it's testament to its universal power. From ancient Chinese proverbs to modern self-help books, humans keep rediscovering the same basic formula because it works, even when we desperately wish it didn't.

Consider how a person builds anything meaningful. A relationship. A career. A skill. The ability to parallel park without causing a small traffic incident. The pattern is always the same: Focused attention over time produces deeper understanding, which in turn enables greater capability. Yet despite this pattern's ubiquity—or perhaps because of it—people often find themselves trying to hack their way around it. Searching for shortcuts, quick fixes, life hacks that promise to revolutionize our existence in just seven minutes a day.

We catch ourselves doing this constantly, even after everything athletics taught us. Recently, Shawn found herself googling "fastest way to learn Spanish," as if there might be some secret technique that would let her bypass the thousands of hours of practice that actual fluency requires.

We all live in an age that promises instant everything: instant coffee, instant messaging, instant gratification. So it's natural to hope for instant mastery too. The internet is full of articles promising to teach you anything "in just 10 steps!" or "in 30 days or less!" as if skills were Amazon Prime deliveries that could show up at your door if you just found the right algorithm.

Mastery is stubbornly analog in a digital world. It refuses to be disrupted, optimized, or compressed into a TikTok video. You can't download it like an app or subscribe to it like a streaming service. It's the one area of human experience that has remained fundamentally unchanged since our ancestors first figured out how to make fire—and probably swore at the process just as much as we do now.

There's something both humbling and liberating about accepting that mastery requires commitment. Humbling because it means acknowledging there are no shortcuts, no matter how many YouTube videos promise otherwise. Liberating because it means the path to excellence is available to anyone willing to put in the work, even if that work occasionally involves crying over a forward roll. But it's also worth saying: Excellence doesn't guarantee recognition, reward, or success in the conventional sense. The real reward is who you become in the process, not just what the world gives you for it.

When Shawn watches young gymnasts now, she often sees them looking for the trick, the special insight that will accelerate their progress. "What's the secret?" they ask, eyes bright with hope. The real secret, if there is one, is simply showing up day after day, ready to do the work—and finding ways to laugh at yourself when you inevitably face-plant into the mat.

In 1885, a German psychologist named Hermann Ebbinghaus performed what might be the most boring experiment in the history of science. He spent years memorizing lists of nonsense syllables—random combinations of letters like "ZOF" and "WUG"—and testing himself at various intervals to see how much he remembered. The result of all this tedium was one of psychology's most important discoveries: the learning curve.

Ebbinghaus found that learning follows a predictable pattern. Progress is rapid at first, then slows dramatically, then plateaus. This pattern holds whether you're memorizing nonsense syllables, learning chess, or mastering a double-twisting double back. It's as if our brains came preprogrammed with this template for acquiring and retaining skills.

But Ebbinghaus discovered something else that speaks directly to the ties between commitment and mastery. He found that the plateau isn't permanent. With continued practice, there are sudden breakthroughs—moments when performance unexpectedly jumps to a new level. These breakthroughs can't be predicted or forced.

It's like hiking the Grand Canyon: For hours, the path seems unchanging, each step leading nowhere new. Then you round a corner and an entirely different vista opens up, revealing layers of beauty that were always there but hidden from view. That's exactly how these breakthroughs emerge: organically from the sustained practice that preceded them.

I experienced these breakthroughs countless times in football, though I didn't have the language for them then. Take long snapping—it sounds simple enough, but perfecting the mechanics of delivering a football 15 yards backward through your legs with pinpoint accuracy while eleven players are charging at you is anything but basic. I would work at refining my snap for weeks or months, feeling stuck, seeing no improvement. My form felt mechanical, my timing off by fractions of seconds that felt like eternities.

Then suddenly, often at some random Tuesday practice when I least expected it, the movement would reorganize itself in my body, becoming smoother, more integrated. My hands would find the laces without conscious thought, my release would sync perfectly with my stance, and the ball would fly back with a consistency that had eluded me for months. These moments felt magical, but they weren't magic. They were the natural result of showing up daily, even—especially—when progress wasn't visible.

The word "mastery" comes from the Latin magister, meaning "teacher" or "chief." But true mastery is about service—to the skill you're developing, the craft you're honing, the art you're creating.

This kind of service requires a commitment that transcends mechanical practice, because at some point you'll want to walk away. The work will stop being exciting and start being uncomfortable. That's the threshold. If you can stay with it, push through the friction, something powerful happens. The challenge begins to shape you. What feels like a problem "out there" is often a lesson trying to be learned in here.

The thing won't fully commit to you until you fully commit to it. And not halfway. Fully. That means prioritizing the commitment over your comfort, your convenience, even your sense of control. True mastery asks you to surrender your ego. The discipline becomes the instructor. The work becomes the curriculum. And you—the one who thought you were mastering the thing—realize you're the one being mastered, shaped, and changed by it.

When I watch truly great performers now—athletes, musicians, surgeons, craftspeople—what strikes me is the quality of their attention. You can see it in a dancer lost in the music, in the way a master carpenter's hands seem to communicate directly with the wood. There's a presence that goes beyond skill. They've developed a relationship with excellence itself.

Perhaps this is what separates competence from mastery: the willingness to commit to the questions as much as the answers, to the process as much as the outcome. Paradoxically, it's often when we release our attachment to achieving mastery that mastery emerges.

This relationship with excellence that Andrew describes has another dimension that's equally important: the relationship with failure. Most people think mastery is about not making mistakes. It's actually the opposite. Mastery is about understanding failure deeply—learning to welcome it, examine it, and maybe even take it out for coffee occasionally (failure always picks up the tab, which is nice).

In gymnastics, we understand this deeply. Every elite gymnast has spent thousands of hours falling—usually in front of coaches, teammates, and sometimes spectators with smartphones ready to immortalize our mishaps for posterity. We fall so often that we develop a connoisseur's appreciation for different types of falls. There's the "almost had it" fall (frustrating), the "not even close" fall (humbling), the "physics has betrayed me" fall (existentially troubling), and my personal favorite, the "I have no idea how I ended up over here" fall (confusing but often hilarious in retrospect, less so in the moment).

What separates those who achieve mastery from those who merely dabble is how they respond when improvement stalls or reverses. The dabbler abandons ship at the first sign of struggle, moving on to the next shiny pursuit like a commitment-phobic butterfly. The master-in-training sighs dramatically, maybe throws a small tantrum, and then gets back to work.

This is where the real mastery begins—in the choppy waters where most people jump overboard. It's about becoming the kind of person who can look failure in the eye and say, "Oh, it's you again. Come on in, let's see what you're here to teach me this time."

This principle extends well beyond sports, often in ways that catch you completely off guard. When Andrew and I embarked on our postathletic careers, we quickly discovered that the same commitment mindset that served us in sports was essential in these new domains. Our first attempts at creating content were, to put it kindly, underwhelming. I still cringe remembering our earliest videos, where we stared awkwardly into the camera with the charisma of two people being held hostage by their own ambition.

Those early days were a master class in failure appreciation. We'd pour hours into creating videos that barely registered any views, refreshing the page obsessively like teenagers checking their social media for likes. Our families seemed to be our only loyal viewers, and even they sometimes forgot to watch. It would have been easy to quit, to assume we weren't cut out for this new arena and retreat to our athletic comfort zones.

But our sports backgrounds had taught us something crucial: The plateau is precisely where most people give up—and precisely where you shouldn't. This is the hidden curriculum of mastery that no one puts in the course catalog. It's learning to find your footing in that uncomfortable space between "I used to be good at something" and "I might eventually be good at this new thing."

Parenting has perhaps been our most humbling arena for applying this mastery mindset. When our daughter was born, all my gymnastics discipline and Andrew's football training suddenly seemed as relevant as a chocolate teapot. No amount of Olympic preparation helps you function on minimal sleep while trying to decipher the needs of a tiny human who communicates primarily through various intensities of crying. I remember looking at Andrew in those early days, both of us shellshocked, wondering if we were even remotely qualified for the life we'd just stepped into.

Yet slowly, I began to recognize familiar patterns from my athletic career. Those moments when you think "I'll never figure this out," right before something clicks. Parenting, like gymnastics, rewards your willingness to adapt when your carefully planned routine goes spectacularly off the rails.

This might be the most surprising aspect of mastery: It requires both unwavering commitment and complete flexibility. You must be simultaneously stubborn about your goals and adaptable about your methods.

In this way, mastery reveals itself as something far more expansive than technical excellence. It's about developing a relationship with the entire journey—the peaks, the valleys, and all those weird detours where you temporarily get lost in someone else's neighborhood. It's about becoming the kind of person who can maintain both serious dedication and the ability to laugh when life inevitably reminds you that you're not quite as in control as you thought.

That journey, though, rarely follows a linear trajectory. There's a phenomenon psychologists call the "J-curve," where performance often dips before it improves. This J-curve is the hidden shape of mastery, the secret topography that every committed practitioner eventually discovers—usually right around the time they start questioning their life choices.

Picture it: You begin learning something new and experience a quick rush of initial progress. The basics come easily. You're energized, optimistic, telling everyone at dinner parties about your exciting new pursuit (and probably being a bit insufferable about it). Then suddenly, the path steepens. What once felt natural now feels awkward. You're over-thinking every movement. You're more aware of your limitations than a teenager looking in a fun-house mirror. Your performance actually declines despite increased effort. Now you're definitely not mentioning it at dinner parties—in fact, you're actively avoiding the topic and maybe those dinner parties altogether.

This is the dip in the J-curve—the place where commitment is truly tested. It's where casual enthu-siasts abandon their pursuits, convinced they've reached their natural ceiling. "I guess I'm just not cut out for this," they tell themselves, moving on to something new, where they can once again experi-ence the dopamine hit of beginner's gains without the discomfort of the dip. We call this the "serial honeymoon approach" to life—always courting, never marrying, chasing new-relationship energy without building anything lasting.

But those committed to mastery recognize the dip for what it truly is: not a warning sign, but a rite of passage. It's the preparation phase you must go through to become the type of person who is capable of the next level. When Shawn was learning complex gymnastics combinations, there was always a phase where the individual elements she had mas-tered separately would fall apart when combined—like watching all your groceries tumble out of their bags just as you reached your front door. When Andrew was perfecting his football techniques, the conscious application of new mechanics temporarily disrupted his natural flow. This seeming regression wasn't failure; it was integration.

In every domain we've entered—athletics, business, relationships, parenting—we've encountered this same pattern. The dip in the J-curve is where your brain and body are reorganizing themselves around deeper principles, where you're moving from conscious competence to unconscious mastery. Think of renovating a house while living in it. There's always that week you're showering in the kitchen, wondering if you've made a terrible mistake.

The dip is also where the truly valuable lessons reveal themselves. In the struggle to integrate new knowledge and skills, you discover nuances invisible to casual practitioners. You develop workarounds for limitations. You invent personal techniques that become part of your unique expression of mastery—like Andrew's elaborate presnap rituals that teammates initially mocked but eventually tried to imitate.

What makes the J-curve so treacherous is its psychological dimension. When you're in the dip, you can't see the upward slope that awaits. There's no guarantee how long the dip will last. This uncertainty tests not just your skill but your faith—faith in the process, faith in your capacity to improve, faith that the discomfort is purposeful rather than pointless.

The commitment that carries you through is a kind of educated trust—faith in the pattern itself. Virtually every master in every field has navigated this same terrain. The concert pianist, the surgeon, the craftsman, the entrepreneur—all have weathered stretches where progress reversed before suddenly accelerating. (A good coach or mentor helps enormously here; more on that later.)

Which is why mastery and commitment can't be separated. Mastery demands resilience—showing up when no one's clapping. Commitment is what builds that resilience, by teaching you to embrace the whole journey, disorienting parts and all, and to find enough humor to stay sane.

Once you understand that the J-curve is a feature, not a bug—that the dip is where transformation actually happens—you begin to glimpse mastery's greatest secret. It's the most surprising discovery of all: The process itself becomes the reward.

Yes, external achievements matter. Medals are nice. Applause feels good. Paychecks are certainly useful, and we're not about to pretend otherwise. But as you progress deeper into any domain of mastery, something curious happens. The external validation, once so crucial, becomes secondary to the internal satisfaction of doing something well for its own sake.

We see this transformation happening in our daughter now as she learns new skills. There's that moment when she figures something out—when she finally manages to zip her own jacket or write her name—and her face lights up with a radiance that has nothing to do with our approval. It's the pure delight of capability, of agency, of having extended the boundaries of what's possible in her world. That intrinsic joy doesn't diminish with age or achievement; it just attaches itself to increasingly complex pursuits.

This is what mastery actually offers: becoming. The person who emerges from a decade of dedicated practice is fundamentally different from the one who started. They see more. They relate to challenge differently. Their capacity for focus and presence has deepened in ways that spill into everything else they do.

We sometimes joke that we both have "commitment personalities." We tend to dive deep when something matters to us—something we've seen modeled by the people who raised, coached, and mentored us. But even with that tendency, staying committed is still a daily choice, and we believe it's a choice available to everyone. We don't have it mastered. We wrestle with doubt, distraction, and the temptation to pull back just like anyone else. What we're learning is that this orientation toward mastery is a posture you can keep practicing. Some people might take to it more naturally, like floating, while others have to learn to swim the hard way. But the waters of deep engagement are there for all of us—as long as we're willing to keep getting wet.

There's something else worth saying: Commitment doesn't have to be grim. Some of the most committed people we know are also the funniest, the most playful, the most alive to the absurdity of existence. Mastery brings a certain lightness—the freedom to play within boundaries you've worked hard to understand. It's the difference between a beginner grimly practicing scales and a master improvising with delight, turning those same scales into something magical.

And you never arrive. There's always another level, another nuance, another dimension. The relationship deepens, evolves, surprises you. Sometimes it frustrates you to the point of wanting to throw things. (We don't recommend this, especially with expensive equipment.) But the commitment itself becomes part of your identity—a thread woven through the fabric of your life.

Which is why we hesitate when people ask for the secret to success. The honest answer is that we're still in it—still learning, still being shaped by the work. There's no clean formula, no hack that skips the hard parts. Wanting the shortcut is like wanting the secret to a great marriage without the arguments, the compromises, the years of showing up.

There are no shortcuts. But there is a secret: The path is the point. The commitment doesn't just lead to mastery—it is the mastery. Once you stop fighting the J-curve and start dancing with it, everything opens up.

THE DISTANCE IS MEASURED IN REPETITIONS. Between a terrified toddler's first forward roll and an Olympic athlete's double-twisting double back: one hundred thousand practice reps of fundamental skills.

MASTERY REMAINS STUBBORNLY ANALOG. You cannot download it, subscribe to it, or hack your way to it. In an age of instant everything, this is strangely reassuring.

PROGRESS FOLLOWS A PREDICTABLE ARC. Fast gains, then slowdowns, then plateaus. Breakthroughs emerge like water finding its way through rock. The J-curve dip, where performance temporarily declines despite increased effort, signals transformation in progress.

FAILURE BECOMES A LANGUAGE. Elite performers develop a connoisseur's appreciation for different types of setbacks. Each one teaches something specific.

THE PROCESS BECOMES THE POINT.
External validation matters early on. But
deep practitioners discover something
else: the intrinsic satisfaction of doing
something well for its own sake.

YOU NEVER ARRIVE. There's always
another level, another nuance. The
relationship deepens and evolves,
surprising you in equal measure.

5

Meaning

When I stepped onto the Olympic podium to receive my gold medal for balance beam, everything looked perfect from the outside. The roar of the Beijing crowd, the flash of cameras, the weight of the medal against my chest—the fairy-tale ending every young gymnast dreams about. My teammates were beaming. My parents were crying in the stands.

But when the scores came in, my coach and I actually giggled. We were proud of the performance, but we both knew it wasn't my best work. Solid, yes. Olympic gold medal–worthy, apparently. But missing something.

To understand why, you have to go back a few days, to the all-around competition. That was my event—the one I'd trained for since I was a little girl in Iowa. Every early morning practice, every missed school dance, every moment of doubt and determination had been building to those routines. When I finished my final pass on floor exercise, I knew I had done the absolute best I was capable of doing. Nastia Liukin earned the gold that night with an incredible performance, and I was genuinely proud of her. I took silver.

Reporters rushed over expecting heartbreak. "How does it feel to lose?" I didn't know how to explain that this "loss" overflowed with meaning. The silver carried its own gold: complete commitment.

That's the difference those two podiums taught me. The beam gold was about excellence in execution. The silver was about excellence in commitment. And standing there, days apart, holding two different medals that felt like two different currencies, I learned something that has shaped everything since: Outcomes don't make meaning. Meaning is made in the daily choice to pour yourself fully into something you believe matters.

This relationship between commitment and meaning shows up everywhere once you start looking for it. It challenges our natural assumption that meaning is something we find rather than something we make—that it exists out there waiting to be discovered, like buried treasure. But the evidence suggests almost the opposite: Meaning emerges most powerfully from the things we commit ourselves to, often in proportion to the depth of that commitment.

What makes this insight so fascinating is that it operates at every scale of human experience—from the Olympic athlete dedicating years to mastering their sport, to the parent patiently nurturing a child's growth, all the way down to the smallest acts of creation and care. This is what behavioral economists Michael Norton, Daniel Mochon, and Dan Ariely noticed in their research: People consistently placed higher value on things they had built themselves, even when the end products were objectively inferior to premade alternatives.

In a series of experiments that gave rise to what they called "the IKEA effect," the researchers discovered that test subjects who assembled their own furniture, folded their own origami, or built their own Lego sets developed a deep emotional connection to these items through the very act of creating them. Most strikingly, participants who created origami valued their amateur creations nearly as much as expertly crafted pieces, despite independent raters judging the amateur work as "nearly worthless crumpled paper."

But here's a crucial detail: This enhanced valuation occurred only when people successfully completed their projects. When participants were prevented from finishing their IKEA storage boxes, or when their origami attempts failed repeatedly and they gave up without achieving a satisfactory result, the effect vanished. This suggests that meaning emerges from the combination of committed engagement carried through to completion.

The IKEA effect helps explain why we cherish the vegetables we grow more than ones we buy, why homemade gifts carry special meaning, and why that imperfect ceramic mug from your child's first pottery class becomes a treasured possession. In each case, the meaning arises not from the object's inherent quality but from the commitment invested in its creation.

This insight has profound implications for how we think about meaning in our lives. When we look at people who report high levels of life satisfaction and sense of purpose, we often find they're not necessarily those who went searching for meaning directly. Instead, they're people who committed themselves fully to something—whether that's a craft, a cause, a community, or a relationship. The meaning emerged as a by-product of their commitment rather than as its direct purpose.

And in that, there's something quietly empowering: By choosing what we commit to, we are, in effect, choosing what will become meaningful. Commitment gives us agency over where meaning can take root, because we shape the conditions under which meaning is allowed to grow.

Let's pause here and acknowledge something important. Talking about "meaning" can feel a bit . . . well, meaningful. Perhaps too meaningful. While we're exploring these connections between commitment and purpose, you might be thinking more practical thoughts, like how to pay the mortgage or whether you remembered to schedule that dentist appointment. Maybe you're wondering if all this philosophizing about meaning is a luxury for people who don't have to worry about whether their car will start tomorrow morning.

And frankly, there's something slightly absurd about analyzing the deep existential significance of assembling IKEA furniture. Even when we venture into weightier territory—like Olympic medals or life-defining achievements—meaning has a way of defying our attempts to pin it down. Ask someone to define exactly what makes something meaningful, and you'll often get the conversational equivalent of a shrug, followed by "I don't know, it just . . . is?"

This elusiveness might explain why we're sometimes tempted to outsource our search for meaning to experts, gurus, or self-help books that promise "7 Life-Changing Secrets to Unlock Your Purpose" (apparently five weren't quite enough). Spoiler alert: If someone claims to have cracked the code of human meaning in bullet points that fit on a bookmark, they're probably selling something other than wisdom.

It's natural to want a road map, especially when the destination feels so important yet so frustratingly vague. We get it. There's something appealingly tidy about the idea that meaning could be delivered like a pizza—hot, fresh, and ready to consume in thirty minutes or less.

But here's what we've learned from our own stumbling journey toward meaning: Sometimes the most profound insights come wrapped in surprisingly mundane packages. Yes, assembling that IKEA bookshelf might just be about having somewhere to put your stuff. That's perfectly fine. But it might also be teaching you something about the satisfaction of creating with your own hands, about following through on a project, about the weird pride that comes from deciphering those wordless instruction manuals.

The meaning is in the commitment to the process, however humble that process might be. It's in the decision to stick with something when it gets frustrating, to keep going when you've got three extra screws and no idea where they're supposed to go.

This is why we're not here to tell you what should be meaningful to you. We're not even here to insist that everything needs to be imbued with deep significance. Sometimes a chair is just a chair, even if you built it yourself and it creaks ominously every time someone sits down. What we are suggesting is that when meaning does emerge in our lives, it often comes through the side door of commitment rather than the front door of conscious seeking.

I think about the question of meaninglessness more than you might expect from someone whose path included some early markers of success. Maybe that's precisely why—because some of my seemingly "successful" moments have felt strangely empty, while other, less obvious victories have overflowed with meaning.

Take my NFL career. I was the top-rated long snapper coming out of college, with multiple teams expressing interest. On paper, I had everything lined up. But unlike my Vanderbilt days, where football shaped my identity and gave structure to my purpose, I drifted through NFL tryouts holding something back.

As I mentioned earlier, I kept one foot out the door—and coaches could tell. Nine teams cut me. Looking back, I get it. They were reading my commitment as much as my skills, and I was giving them plenty to read. Partial commitment is visible. It leaks.

I've since discovered the flip side. My most meaningful moments have come from diving fully into something uncertain, like learning to fly.

Aviation might seem like a random hobby until you understand what drew me to it. Flying demands total commitment. Every preflight check, every weather assessment, every landing requires complete presence. There's something deeply satisfying about an endeavor where "close enough" can kill you. The meticulous attention aviation demands—checking systems, monitoring conditions, making constant microadjustments—creates a focused engagement that generates its own meaning.

What I've learned is that meaninglessness often shows up wearing a success costume. It's what happens when we try to skip the hard part of investing ourselves fully in something, when we attempt to harvest meaning without first planting the seeds of genuine engagement. The more you try to shortcut your way to it, the more likely it is to elude you entirely.

Andrew's experience with meaninglessness in the NFL points to something much larger than one person's relationship with professional football. Scientists studying human well-being have uncovered a fascinating pattern that appears whenever good fortune arrives without the accompanying investment of effort and commitment—a pattern that shows up everywhere from lottery winners to trust fund kids to people who get promoted because their boss's nephew needed a job.

Consider a curious finding from studies of what psychologists call "earned success" versus "windfall gains." When researchers examine how people value and use money they've earned through sustained effort compared with equivalent amounts they've received through inheritance or other unearned sources, a fascinating pattern emerges. People tend to be more careful, thoughtful, and ultimately more satisfied with resources they've accumulated through their own sustained effort. (Apparently, money you've sweated for feels different in your wallet than money that just showed up one day like an unexpected houseguest.)

This phenomenon has caught the attention of researchers studying human motivation and well-being. The distinction isn't about the money itself—a dollar is a dollar, after all—but about the psychological meaning we attach to things we've earned through committed engagement over time. Even when the end result is identical, the path to achieving it fundamentally shapes how we experience it.

This mirrors what psychologists call "the effort paradox": The very things that make experiences challenging often make them more meaningful. Mountain climbers, for instance, consistently rate their expeditions as more meaningful when they're more difficult—even though, in the moment, they might desperately wish for an easier path and possibly question their life choices. Think about older couples telling parents with newborns "you're gonna miss this," even when those parents look like they haven't slept since the Mesozoic era.

The same pattern appears in studies of education: When students engage with difficult material and eventually master it, the learning proves more durable and transferable than when they breeze through without effort. The struggle itself—that cognitive wrestling with challenging concepts—creates deeper understanding and stronger retention in ways that easy victories simply can't match.

Meaning emerges from committed engagement with challenges over time. This helps explain why life's freebies can feel oddly unfulfilling—the victory achieved through luck, the relationship that comes easily. Welcome? Sure. But missing something essential.

The research suggests that meaning comes from the story we write through sustained effort. This story doesn't need to be epic. It might be finally getting your sourdough to rise. Training a stubborn puppy. Coaxing your garden through a difficult season. Finishing a quilt your grandmother started. What matters is that we're active authors of our own experience, adding our own chapters to the book.

Meaning has a habit of showing up where you least expect it. The parent who finds profound purpose? Usually happens somewhere between the seventeenth diaper change and the third sleepless night, not during some reverent meditation on the miracle of life. The craftsperson who discovers their calling? More likely while cursing at a stubborn block of marble than during a vision quest. The volunteer who builds deep connection? Probably while making terrible coffee for the hundredth time, not while contemplating the abstract nature of community.

Meaning has terrible timing. You go looking for it with your spiritual metal detector, and it hides. You get busy doing something that matters to you—really doing it, day after day, even when it's boring or hard or thankless—and meaning taps you on the shoulder, like "Oh hey, I've been here the whole time."

Which brings us to the million-dollar question: If meaning comes through commitment, what exactly should we commit to?

In a world that offers everything, how do we choose something? The modern temptation is to dabble, commit to nothing, and keep our options open like a twenty-four-hour diner. But that strategy works great for breakfast foods, less great for building a meaningful life.

Maybe we're asking the wrong question. Instead of "Where can I find meaning?" try "What am I willing to show up for, even when it's annoying?" That shift changes the whole game. Suddenly you're not waiting for meaning to arrive like an Amazon package. You're creating the conditions in which it might grow.

Your answer won't match anyone else's. Maybe you'll find meaning in teaching kids who'd rather be anywhere else. Maybe in writing code that makes people's lives marginally less irritating. Maybe in keeping bees (they're surprisingly philosophical, those bees). The specific choice matters less than whether you stick around long enough to get past the honeymoon phase.

Meaning isn't hiding in some other life you haven't found yet. It's here, in this one, waiting for you to stop swiping left on your actual commitments and finally say yes.

TROPHIES CAN FEEL HOLLOW. A gold medal won with partial commitment can feel emptier than a silver earned through full devotion. External success and internal meaning follow different logics.

WE MAKE MEANING MORE THAN WE FIND IT. The IKEA effect: People value what they build themselves, even when objectively inferior to premade alternatives. Meaning emerges from committed engagement.

EFFORT CHANGES VALUE. Money earned through sustained work feels different than a windfall. Material struggled over sticks longer than material breezed through. The path shapes the destination.

MEANING SNEAKS UP ON YOU. Chase it directly and it recedes. Show up faithfully to something you care about, and it emerges on its own schedule.

DAILY ACTS FORGE SIGNIFICANCE. Meaning accumulates through consistency, through pushing past the temptation to quit when excitement fades. The dramatic moments are just visible peaks of quieter mountains.

What

So here's where things get interesting—and slightly terrifying.

By now, you've seen how commitment can transform your life in ways that sound almost too good to be true. Calm instead of chaos. Joy that deepens rather than fades. The ability to see possibilities others miss entirely. Mastery that feels less like work and more like play. And meaning that emerges not from searching for it, but from the beautiful act of showing up fully to something that matters.

All of which brings us to the question that's probably been nagging at you since chapter 1: "Okay, I'm convinced. But commit to what, exactly?"

This is where the rubber meets the road, where inspiration crashes headlong into the practical reality of having to make actual decisions about your actual life. Because while we've spent five chapters showing you what commitment can do, we haven't yet tackled the trickier puzzle of figuring out what deserves your devotion in the first place.

This matters enormously. Commitment without wisdom is like a sports car without a steering wheel—lots of power, but you're probably going to end up in a ditch. We've all seen people pour themselves completely into relationships that drain them, careers that crush their souls, or causes that prove to be mirages dressed up as missions.

The next five chapters are about developing what we call "commitment intelligence"—the ability to distinguish between worthy devotions and attractive distractions, between sustainable paths and dead ends disguised as dreams. We'll explore how to read the clues your life is already giving you, how to identify the values that should guide your choices, and how to navigate the complex territory of love and relationships.

We'll also tackle one of commitment's cardinal truths: Sometimes the best choice is the one you can't fully see yet, the path that reveals itself only through the act of walking it. And yes, we'll address the elephant in the room—what happens when it's time to change course, when commitment becomes a prison instead of liberation?

Because here's what we've learned: In a world of infinite options, not choosing is still a choice—it's just a choice that guarantees you'll stay exactly where you are. The real question is how to choose wisely, how to bet your precious time and energy on things that will reward your devotion rather than waste it.

Ready to figure out what deserves the gift of your full attention? Let's dive in.

6

Clues

When Kobe Bryant committed himself to becoming the greatest basketball player of all time, he said something striking: "The world became my library." Ballet taught him footwork. Philosophy sharpened his mindset. Every experience became material for his craft.

But Bryant already knew what he was looking for. What if you don't? What if you're wandering the stacks, pulling books off shelves at random, unsure which section even belongs to you?

This is where many of us find ourselves—convinced that commitment matters, but paralyzed by the question of what deserves our devotion. Everyone else seems to be confidently checking out their life's work while you're still browsing.

Sometimes this paralysis shows up in small ways: the unused hobby supplies gathering dust in the corner, the half-finished online courses multiplying in your browser bookmarks, the exercise equipment that's become an expensive clothes rack. Other times it manifests more profoundly: the career that never quite feels right, the relationship that stays perpetually casual, the life that feels like a rough draft waiting for its final form—or at least a decent second draft.

We understand. We've both had our share of false starts and uncertain paths. Even after achieving what might look like clear direction from the outside—Olympic medals, NFL career—we've found ourselves asking the same questions many of you are asking: What next? What deserves my full attention? What should I commit to when the obvious answer isn't obvious anymore?

All the benefits we've explored—the calm, the joy, the depth, the mastery, the meaning—are available only if you actually commit to something. It's like having a key that can open any door, but first you have to choose which door you want to walk through. The most beautiful key in the world is useless if you spend your whole life standing in the hallway admiring it.

In the pages that follow, we'll share a series of questions and exercises designed to help you uncover the commitments that might be waiting for you. Some will be practical, others playful. Some might lead you to grand ambitions, while others might guide you to quiet, personal devotions—like

Shawn's recent journey into making sourdough bread, which has unexpectedly opened doors to a world of possibilities (and carbohydrates).

Think of this chapter as a kind of treasure hunt, where the X on the map marks not a single destination but rather a constellation of possibilities. We'll help you look for clues in your past, your present habits, and your secret wishes. We'll explore what your spending patterns might reveal about your hidden interests, what your family history might suggest about your natural inclinations, and what your idle daydreams might be trying to tell you about your future.

The goal is to discover paths worth walking, interests worth exploring, passions worth pursuing with the full force of your attention. The first step is acknowledging that uncertainty is fine. The second is looking for clues. The third? That's what the rest of this chapter is for.

What's remotely interesting to you?

A few years ago, I sat in our living room with a family coach who asked me what seemed like a simple question: "What are your hobbies?"

I stared back at him blankly, like he'd just asked me to solve quantum physics using interpretive

dance. For six years, I had been in the thick of baby life—pregnant, postpartum, or caring for young children. My hobbies at that point consisted of things like "successfully drinking coffee while it was still warm" and "going to the bathroom alone." When I tried to answer his question, I realized I couldn't name a single hobby that was truly mine and didn't involve keeping tiny humans alive.

This moment of recognition might sound familiar to you. Perhaps your specifics are different—maybe you've been consumed by a demanding career, or caring for aging parents, or pursuing a singular goal that left room for little else. But the sensation of looking up from a period of intense focus and realizing you've lost touch with other parts of yourself? That's surprisingly universal.

The coach, Don, gave me an assignment that I now pass on to you: "Write the world's longest list of anything that sounds even remotely interesting to you." Don't worry about practicality. Don't filter for skill level or time commitment. Don't even worry if it sounds ridiculous. Just let your mind wander and your pen move.

Horseback riding? Write it down. Drawing? Add it to the list. Reading mystery novels? Yes. Lighting bonfires? Why not. Learning to juggle? Absolutely. Becoming a professional cheese taster? Sure, that's a thing that exists somewhere.

The beauty of this exercise lies in its permission to dream widely, like opening all the windows in a house that's been closed up for too long. For me, this list became a sort of treasure map. Among dozens of possibilities—some practical, some wildly ambitious, some involving way more physical coordination than I realistically possessed—I wrote down "sourdough bread making."

Now, I should mention that at the time, my relationship with baking was . . . complicated. I was the person who could burn water and had once created what could only be described as "concrete cookies" for a school fundraiser. But something about the idea of sourdough intrigued me.

Maybe it was the ancient tradition of it, the fact that people had been doing this for thousands of years with nothing but flour, water, and patience. Or maybe it was just the romantic notion of having a living starter that I could name and talk to (don't judge me, I was sleep-deprived).

It took two years before I actually bought the supplies. Two years of that list sitting in a drawer while I told myself I was "too busy" and "not the baking type." Then a few more months of the supplies sitting on my counter while I worked up the courage to begin, convinced I would somehow manage to kill what is essentially immortal bacteria.

But when I finally did start, the rhythm of feeding the starter every day became meditative rather than burdensome. The process of kneading dough—which I had expected to find tedious— turned out to be surprisingly therapeutic. And the satisfaction of pulling a perfect loaf from the oven? Well, let's just say I may have taken more photos of bread than most people take of their children.

What started as a simple hobby has opened up an entire world I never knew existed. I've learned about fermentation science, discovered local grain farmers, and yes, I've started planning a chicken coop, because apparently once you go down the homemade rabbit hole, fresh eggs are the logical next step. From sourdough to farm-fresh eggs—it's a path I never would have predicted, but it feels right. It feels like me, even if past-me would be very confused by present-me's enthusiasm for carbohydrates and poultry.

The point isn't that you need to become an amateur baker or urban farmer (though if you do, I have some excellent starter recipes to share). The point is that sometimes our next meaningful commitment is already whispering to us—we just need to give ourselves permission to listen.

So grab a pen. Make your list. Don't judge what appears on it. You're simply opening a conversation with yourself. And who knows? You might just discover that the thing you're meant to commit to has been waiting patiently for you to notice it all along.

Who do you look up to? There's a revealing question we often forget to ask ourselves: Who do you admire, and more importantly, what are they committed to?

Our admiration often contains hidden messages about our potential commitments. When we find ourselves drawn to certain people—whether they're in our immediate circle or dominating our social media feeds with their annoyingly perfect lives—it's worth paying attention to what specifically captures our imagination.

Do you envy a neighbor's job because it gives them flexibility, or because they work with a large team? If you're jealous of a friend's marriage, is it their romantic date nights, or the way they laugh easily and seem deeply at ease with each other? These details matter. They point not to what we lack, but to what we long for—and what we might be ready to commit to ourselves.

The key is to look beyond the Instagram-worthy achievements to understand the underlying commitments that made them possible. That friend whose garden you admire while your own houseplants stage regular revolts? Look closer. Maybe what truly draws you isn't their perfect tomatoes or uncanny ability to keep things alive, but their patient dedication to nurturing something over time, watching it grow from seed to harvest.

The colleague whose presentations always captivate the room while yours inspire people to suddenly remember urgent emails that absolutely must be checked immediately? Perhaps it's public speaking that interests you, but it could also be their commitment to crafting compelling narratives and making complex ideas accessible.

This form of observation is about recognition—seeing in others the hints of what might bring us fulfillment too. Sometimes we spot in someone else's life a pattern we'd like to weave into our own, even if in a completely different form.

Think of it as borrowing someone else's flashlight to illuminate your own path. You don't have to walk exactly where they walked, but their light might help you see the way forward.

So who catches your attention? Who makes you think "I want some of whatever they've got"? And what are they actually committed to that creates that sense of fulfillment you're drawn to?

Sometimes the path to meaningful commitment starts with a simple question: What makes you deeply uncomfortable?

I discovered this truth last year when my friend Matt and I began sending each other weekly challenges designed specifically to push us out of our comfort zones. Every Wednesday, we'd take turns assigning each other tasks that made us squirm—physically, emotionally, and mentally. It was like having a personal trainer for your psychological growth, except instead of making your muscles sore, we were making our egos cringe.

One week, the challenge was to sit down and draw our surroundings for ten minutes. Sounds simple enough, right? Just you, a pencil, and whatever happens to be in front of you. But for someone who hasn't picked up a pencil to sketch since childhood—and whose artistic peak was probably stick figures that looked vaguely human—it was surprisingly intimidating. The discomfort came from confronting our own awkwardness, our own rusty creativity, and the humbling reality that our artistic skills had apparently been in hibernation for decades.

I remember sitting there, staring at a coffee mug and a stack of books, thinking, "How hard can this be?" Turns out, very hard. My drawing looked like it had been done by someone wearing oven mitts during an earthquake. But there was something oddly liberating about creating something terrible and being okay with it.

Another week, we had to write letters to ourselves on our wedding days—I was already married; my friend wasn't. The exercise forced us to look both backward and forward, to examine our choices and dreams from different vantage points. It was uncomfortable in that peculiar way that only real self-reflection can be, like emotional archaeology.

Writing to my past self felt strange—part advice

column, part time-travel fantasy. What would I tell that nervous guy standing at the altar? What did I know now that I wished I'd known then? It was the kind of exercise that makes you realize how much you've grown without noticing.

Some challenges were more physical: waking up before dawn for an ice bath, with the rule that we had to submerge ourselves within minutes of our alarm going off. No time to overthink it, no room for hesitation, and definitely no time to talk ourselves out of it while standing there in our underwear questioning our life choices. Just pure, shocking commitment to the uncomfortable—literally shocking, in the case of the ice bath.

I'll spare you the details of my reaction to that first plunge, but let's just say it involved sounds I didn't know I was capable of making and a vocabulary that would make a sailor blush.

What we discovered through this process went beyond building resilience or proving something to ourselves (though we definitely proved we were both slightly unhinged). It was about mapping the edges of our comfort zones, about understanding where we naturally pull back and why. Because often, in that space of resistance, we find clues about what we need to explore more deeply.

Think about it: What if the things that make you most uncomfortable are actually signposts pointing toward potential commitments? What if your resistance to public speaking is an invitation to explore what scares you about it? What if your discomfort with creativity is a door that's been locked so long you forgot you had the key?

The point isn't to make yourself miserable for sport (we're not masochists, despite evidence to the contrary). It's to recognize that discomfort can be a compass, pointing us toward areas of potential growth and meaningful commitment. Sometimes, the very things we avoid most steadfastly are the things that, if embraced, could lead to our most significant transformations.

What makes you uncomfortable enough that you might need to explore it? What makes you squirm in a way that suggests there's something important hiding behind that resistance?

What's hiding in your family tree?

Sometimes the clues to what we should commit to are hiding in plain sight, woven into our family histories like a genetic treasure map nobody bothers to read until they're having an existential crisis.

I discovered this while reflecting on my relationship with adrenaline and movement. My father was what you might generously call an adrenaline junkie—racing motorcycles, sprint cars, three-wheelers, basically anything with wheels and a flagrant disregard for reasonable safety margins. He lived for that rush of controlled danger, the kind that made my mother age prematurely and invest heavily in good health insurance.

As a child, I was constantly in the emergency room, because I was utterly convinced I could fly. I'd launch myself off the entertainment center with the confidence of someone who had clearly never heard of gravity, or leap from the stairwell like I was auditioning for a superhero movie. The ER staff knew us by name. "Oh, it's the flying Johnson kid again. . . ."

Everyone laughed and said I'd inherited my dad's adrenaline-seeking side. What none of us realized was that this same impulse—this desire to fly, to push boundaries, to find that perfect blend of risk and control—would find its ultimate expression in Olympic gymnastics. The flips and twists that would eventually earn me a gold medal were just a more disciplined version of those early living-room launches. Better landing mats. Judges holding up scores. Fewer parental heart attacks.

Looking back, it's almost comically obvious. Of course the kid who spent her childhood trying to defy gravity would end up in a sport that's basically organized defiance of gravity.

Each family passes down physical traits like your grandmother's nose, personality quirks like your uncle's unfortunate tendency toward dad jokes, and proclivities that can take entirely new forms in each generation. My father's love of speed became my love of flight. Same fundamental drive, different expression.

Look at your own family tree. What patterns emerge? Maybe your grandfather did a seven-minute jogging-in-place routine in his closet every morning (home gyms before they were trendy), and your father pounded the pavement at dawn regardless of weather. Endurance might be in your DNA—a physiological advantage passed down through generations. Your version might be cycling, hiking, or hot yoga. Some habits are universally beneficial, but others are uniquely suited to your build, wiring, and temperament. The goal is to notice what your lineage is quietly telling you you're built for.

These inherited inclinations are starting points for exploration—clues on your journey, suggesting directions worth investigating, even if the ultimate destination is entirely your own.

What potential commitments are already staring you in the face?

Sometimes discovering what to commit to means becoming a detective of your own present. The clues are already there, scattered throughout your life like breadcrumbs—in your calendar, in your credit card statements, and, yes, in your slightly embarrassing browser history.

Think about where your money naturally flows when you're not overthinking. That monthly donation to the local animal shelter you never skip, even when you're eating ramen for the third time this week. The art supplies you keep buying despite having no time for hobbies. The cooking gadgets multiplying in your kitchen drawers. These are clues: Your money is voting for your interests, even when your conscious mind is still figuring out what those interests actually are.

Your calendar tells a more honest story than your vision board ever could. Forget what you say you value—look at where your hours actually go. Maybe you wake up early to read. You're not a morning person. You're not even a book person. But there you are, up before dawn with a novel. That's data.

Perhaps you always find time to help friends troubleshoot their tech problems, even when you're supposedly too busy to answer your own emails. Or you might notice that whenever there's a community event that needs volunteers—the kind where you get to work behind the scenes rather than make small talk—you're mysteriously able to rearrange your schedule to help out.

These patterns are authenticity leaking through the cracks of your routine, like water finding its way through concrete.

The key is to look at your life with a detective's

eye. What books do you grab first at the library, and which ones do you abandon after three pages? Which conversations make you lose track of time so completely that you realize you've been standing in the grocery store produce section for forty-five minutes discussing sourdough starter maintenance? What topics send you down internet rabbit holes at midnight, emerging three hours later wondering how you went from looking up a recipe to reading about the mating habits of deep-sea creatures?

These are compass points indicating directions worth exploring more deeply. Your life is already telling you a story about what matters to you, narrating itself through your choices both big and small. The question is: Are you listening, or are you too busy wondering why you don't have a clear life plan like everyone else seems to?

Try this: Take out your phone right now and look at your photos from the past month. What patterns do you see? Are they mostly of food, your pets looking judgmental, sunsets that never quite capture how beautiful they looked in person, or something else entirely? What moments did you consider worth capturing and preserving?

Sometimes our most genuine commitments are hiding in plain sight in our camera roll, just waiting for us to connect the dots between that picture of your neighbor's garden and your secret desire to grow something yourself.

So what story is your life already telling you? And

more importantly, are you ready to stop ignoring the plot and start paying attention to what you're actually writing?

W hat's the smallest commitment you could keep?

Sometimes the biggest obstacle to meaningful commitment isn't a lack of options—it's a lack of confidence in our ability to commit at all. We look at the mountain ahead and forget that every climber started with a single step, probably while wearing completely inappropriate footwear and questioning their sanity.

Think of commitment as a muscle that needs training, rather than a character trait you either have or don't (like the ability to parallel park or remember where you put your keys). You wouldn't walk into a gym for the first time and try to dead-lift three hundred pounds—well, you could, but the only thing you'd be committing to is a lengthy relationship with a physical therapist. Similarly, you don't have to start your commitment journey by pledging your life to a grand cause or making some irrevocable decision about your future that sounds like it belongs in a dramatic movie trailer.

Instead, consider a "practice of commitment"—which sounds very official but is really just a fancy way of saying "start small before you embarrass yourself." Begin with something small enough to be manageable but significant enough to matter. Something that stretches you just enough to build your commitment muscles, but not so much that you'll strain them and spend the next week complaining about your poor life choices.

The size of the commitment matters less than the act of seeing it through. It might be as simple as committing to read for fifteen minutes every morning (yes, social media scrolling counts as reading, but maybe aim a little higher), or to call a friend every Sunday instead of just thinking about calling them while feeling vaguely guilty, or to learn one new chord on the guitar each week (even though your current repertoire consists of three chords played with the enthusiasm of someone defusing a bomb).

These may seem like modest aims—the kind of goals that wouldn't impress anyone at a dinner party—but they serve a crucial purpose: They teach you that you can commit. They build your confidence in your own word to yourself, which, let's be honest, might need some rebuilding if you're anything like the rest of us who have made and broken approximately 847 promises to ourselves about exercising regularly.

Each small commitment you keep becomes evidence that you can keep bigger ones. Each morning that you actually do read for those fifteen minutes instead of immediately reaching for your phone proves that you're capable of following through. Each weekly call you make demonstrates that you can maintain a rhythm of dedication, even when your friend inevitably answers with "I was just thinking about you!"

This isn't about starting small and staying small forever, like someone who only ever orders appetizers because they're afraid of commitment to a full entrée. It's about starting small to grow strong. Just as a bodybuilder gradually increases their weights (and their protein shake consumption and their tendency to grunt while lifting), you can gradually increase the scope and scale of your commitments as your confidence grows.

Remember: Every master chef once burned toast. Every marathon runner started by running around the block and probably questioning whether they were having a heart attack or were just really out of shape. Every great commitment begins with a small promise kept, usually when no one else is watching and there's no external reward except the quiet satisfaction of doing what you said you'd do.

What small commitment could you make today that would help you believe in your ability to make bigger ones tomorrow? What's your equivalent of successfully boiling water—modest enough to be achievable, but meaningful enough to matter?

As we close this chapter, you might be feeling both excited and overwhelmed. Perhaps you've discovered that your calendar reveals an unexpected passion for teaching others, or your family history hints at a creative streak you've never fully explored. Maybe you're intrigued by the idea of seeking out discomfort, or you've identified someone whose commitments you'd like to study more closely. The possibilities might feel endless—and in a way, they are.

But this isn't about committing to everything. Think of all these questions and exercises as a constellation of stars in your night sky. Some will shine brighter than others. Some might form patterns that point in a particular direction. Your task isn't to follow every star, but to notice which ones keep drawing your gaze back to them.

The questions we've explored—about your spending patterns, your family history, your admirations, your discomforts, your natural inclinations—are really just different lenses through which to view your life. Each one offers a slightly different perspective, and together they can help you triangulate your position and possible direction.

In the next few chapters, we'll explore how to evaluate the commitments you're considering, how to know when a commitment is worth pursuing more deeply, and how to recognize when it might be time to let go. But for now, sit with the questions we've explored. Let them percolate. Notice which ones keep bubbling up to the surface of your mind.

Take out a notebook or open a new document on your phone. Start making your lists—of interests, of admirations, of patterns you've noticed, of discomforts worth exploring. Let yourself dream a little bigger than feels comfortable. Remember that every significant commitment started as a simple possibility, a quiet what-if.

The answers will come. They might not arrive all at once, and they might not arrive in the form you expect. But by asking these questions, by paying attention to the breadcrumbs your life has been leaving, you're already on your way to discovering what's worth committing to.

START WITH THE LONGEST POSSIBLE LIST. Write down anything that captures your imagination. Don't filter for practicality. Permission to dream widely opens honest conversations with yourself.

STUDY YOUR ADMIRATIONS. The people who consistently capture your attention reveal clues about what might fulfill you, even if expressed in completely different domains.

USE DISCOMFORT AS A COMPASS. Resistance often points toward growth. The things that make you most uncomfortable may be invitations worth accepting.

YOUR RECEIPTS REVEAL YOUR VALUES. Spending patterns, calendar habits, browser history—these show what you naturally prioritize when you're not overthinking. Your real commitments are hiding in plain sight.

BUILD THE MUSCLE WITH SMALL WEIGHTS. Start with the smallest sustainable commitment. Every promise kept becomes evidence you can keep bigger ones.

YOUR FIRST COMMITMENT ISN'T FOREVER. Give yourself permission to start somewhere imperfect, learn from what doesn't work, and grow gradually into deeper devotions.

7

Values

The first time someone suggested I figure out my values, I thought it was the most pointless exercise imaginable. And yet I couldn't stop thinking about it.

I was still playing football. My coach had been talking about team values during practice. That evening, I turned to Shawn and blurted out: "We need to do values." No context. No explanation.

She looked at me blankly, but being Shawn, she was game. So there we sat, both of us hunched over our laptops, literally googling "list of values." A black-and-white PDF of about two hundred words appeared on our screens—loyalty, honesty, respect, achievement, adventure—all these obviously good traits listed in neat rows. We skimmed through and picked the ones that sounded nice; the whole process took maybe five minutes.

It felt ridiculous. What was the point? Who wouldn't choose respect or honesty? Why would anyone need to write down that they value trustworthiness? It seemed like a corporate exercise that had somehow leaked into real life, a thing people talk about that doesn't actually impact anything.

But something strange happened. We kept coming back to it.

A year later, we tried again, this time spending an hour on our back porch. Two years after that, we devoted three entire days to the exercise. With each iteration, the values we identified—playfulness, curiosity, togetherness, faithfulness, and generous stewardship—became less like nice-sounding words and more like a navigational system for our lives.

I realize now what we were doing in those earliest, awkward attempts: We were trying to articulate the hidden operating system running in our minds. We were naming the invisible forces guiding our decisions, our reactions, our instinctive pulls toward certain choices and away from others.

Values represent the underlying principles that are already at work in your life, whether you've named them or not. The person who loses sleep when they've been lied to? That reveals something about how they value truth. The person who feels most alive in a group rather than alone? That says something about how they value community.

Commitment without clarity about your values is like setting sail without knowing your destination. You might make progress, but in what direction? Toward what end? I've discovered that the clearest, most energizing commitments in my life are the ones aligned with the values I hold most deeply.

In this chapter, I want to invite you into what initially felt like an empty exercise but has become one of the most clarifying practices in our lives.

Think of values as a bouncer at your life's door. Every day, a line forms: opportunities, requests, distractions, all dressed up and promising a good time. Your values decide who gets in. They transform the overwhelming question of "What should I commit to?" into the much clearer "Does this align with what matters most to me?"

When we were younger, we could afford to drift, to experiment freely. In our twenties, having no commitments felt like exploration. In our thirties, we found ourselves deeply committed to people, jobs, and ideas that didn't actually reflect who we were. The cost of misaligned commitment grows as we age. The goal is to ensure our commitments reflect our deepest values.

We learned this through our own difficult choices. When the producers of **The Amazing Race** invited us to participate, we were initially thrilled.

Free travel around the world. Television exposure. Adventure. A substantial prize if we won. On the surface, an obvious yes.

But filtered through our value of "togetherness," it became an equally obvious no. The filming schedule would separate us from our young children for weeks. The excitement of racing across continents paled against bedtime stories and morning pancakes. We declined—a decision that would have been agonizing without clear values.

Values can also illuminate when well-intentioned commitments undermine what matters most. Andrew found himself in three different men's groups, all wonderful communities filled with great people. But the combined schedule had him leaving home at six o'clock two mornings a week and missing dinner and bedtime two evenings a month.

What began as a commitment to help our family—seeking wisdom that would make him a better husband and father—was working against our core value of togetherness. When Shawn pointed this out, it sparked an important conversation. "You're doing Bible studies because you want to help the family," she noted, "but in doing them, you're taking away what matters most to us."

This is the hidden superpower of well-articulated values: They reduce decision fatigue. They create clarity in the fog of options. They help you hold each potential commitment up and ask: Does this align with what matters to me? If not, thank it politely and let it go.

We get it. This whole thing can feel silly.

The idea of sitting down with a laptop, googling "list of values," and picking through words like "integrity," "excellence," and "authenticity" feels about as natural as wearing someone else's shoes. It's awkward. It's contrived. It's the kind of exercise that makes you glance over your shoulder to check if anyone's watching you do something so embarrassingly earnest.

Our first attempt took about five minutes and felt completely pointless. We picked words that sounded nice—who doesn't value honesty or respect?—and then promptly forgot about them. It was like those corporate retreats where everyone agrees that "communication" matters, then returns to their desks to continue not communicating.

But the awkwardness doesn't invalidate the importance.

Most transformative practices feel strange at first. Meditation feels ridiculous until suddenly it doesn't. Exercise feels pointless until one day you realize you've changed. Learning to play an instrument is all painful fumbling until, suddenly, you're making music.

Defining your values is no different. The discomfort you feel is just resistance to self-examination. It's the initial friction that precedes clarity.

After the initial awkwardness, the exercise stops being about nice-sounding words and starts revealing the actual architecture of your choices. You begin to notice patterns—the consistent reasons behind your strongest reactions, your deepest satisfactions, your most persistent frustrations.

You might discover that what you thought was anxiety about a career choice is actually tension between your unspoken value of security and your equally important value of growth. Or that your chronic exhaustion stems from constantly saying yes to requests that violate your core value of autonomy.

So we invite you to embrace the awkwardness. Print out a list of values if you need somewhere to start. Pick the ones that resonate, even if you feel a bit self-conscious doing so. Talk about them with someone who knows you well. Notice which ones make you nod in recognition versus which ones just sound nice.

The initial discomfort is temporary, but the clarity it generates can guide decades of decisions. In a world that constantly pulls us in opposing directions, that clarity becomes essential. Who knows? Someday, you might even find yourself spending an entire weekend creating your values, debating with your spouse about whether "curiosity" is more or less accurate for your family values than "inquisitive." (Ask us how we know.)

My first real encounter with values came from my papa, who used to say, "Do things with such excellence that you'd be proud to sign your name to them." I was maybe twelve years old, and I didn't fully understand what he meant. But that phrase—the first directive I had as a compass—lodged somewhere in my brain.

In 2011, Shawn and I tried to formalize our values together for the first time. We sat on the couch with our laptops, googled "list of values," and found one of those images with a hundred words arranged in a neat grid. We went through and picked the ones that sounded important, the ones coaches and teachers had always talked about, the ones we aspired to embody. We ended up with this list: Adventure, Altruism, Authenticity, Community, Courage, Excellence, Faith, Family, Generosity, Gratitude, Humility, Joy, Love, Perseverance, Teamwork.

Fifteen values. So many that each one became irrelevant. We'd created a list of who we wanted to be, not who we actually were.

Two years later, I tried again on my own. This time I borrowed from our football team's values, which were painted on the wall in bold letters: POSITIVE ATTITUDE. GREAT WORK ETHIC. COMPETE IN EVERYTHING YOU DO. MUST BE WILLING TO

SACRIFICE. They sounded important. They looked official. But they were someone else's words for someone else's purpose.

Then in 2017, we took another pass. We were hiring our first employee and realized we needed company values. Shawn typed them up beautifully—all caps, perfectly spaced:

RESPECT: A regard for each individual's talents, abilities, and responsibilities.

PASSION & PURPOSE: Passionately driven by a greater purpose. Driven by a "why" and not a "what."

DRIVE: Each member of our team should have an innate urge to strive toward a common goal.

RESOLUTE: Admirably purposeful, determined, and unwavering.

INTEGRITY: Being honest and having high moral standards inside and outside the business.

TRANSPARENCY: Honesty and accountability in the good and the bad.

Looking back at these attempts now, we smile. Each one was sincere. Each one taught us something. But they were values we thought we should have rather than values we'd discovered through living. The specificity and personal resonance that would actually guide our decisions . . . that came later.

This is why values discovery isn't a one-and-done exercise. It's an iterative journey that deepens as you grow. What began as a googled list eventually evolved into something real—the principles that now serve as our family's compass. But it took years of living, failing, and paying attention to get there.

It's one thing to say "we value curiosity" on a piece of paper; it's another thing entirely to see that value walking around in tiny sneakers, asking questions that make strangers simultaneously uncomfortable and delighted.

One unexpected joy has been watching our three-year-old internalize our family values in ways we never explicitly taught him. Apparently, we didn't need to give him lectures on the importance of curiosity. He was taking mental notes all along.

One evening, we were at a Mexican restaurant when our son started making eye contact with strangers across the room. Before I could even reach for the chips and salsa, he was shouting at a man across the restaurant with the confidence of a tiny talk-show host: "WHAT'S YOUR NAME?" The poor man looked startled but then smiled. "Louis," he replied. Our son's face lit up like he'd just discovered a new species. "WHAT'S YOUR LAST NAME?" he continued, completely oblivious to the unwritten rule that restaurant conversations should be confined to your own table.

I caught Andrew's eye in that moment of parental crossroads— do we shush him and apologize profusely, or let this play out? We recognized what was happening: Our little guy was living out our family value of curiosity with zero filters and maximum volume.

Instead of shutting it down, we encouraged the questions. And what happened next was remarkable—the restaurant atmosphere shifted. People smiled, engaged, exchanged stories. The invisible walls between tables temporarily dissolved.

Curiosity has shaped our adult lives too. It's why Andrew got his pilot's license and went back to school. It's why we're constantly trying new recipes and learning new skills. We don't just want to follow the everyday routine; we want to keep exploring, asking questions, discovering—even if that occasionally means loudly interrogating strangers about their life choices over tacos.

What's fascinating is that we didn't consciously choose "curiosity" because it sounded impressive on paper. We recognized it as something already running in the background of our lives, like essential software. Naming it simply allowed us to celebrate it more intentionally and create more opportunities for it to flourish. It also helped us understand why certain activities energize rather than deplete us, and why some of our happiest family memories involve discovering something new together.

When your values are truly aligned with who you are, they feel like the most natural expression of your authentic self—even when that expression comes through a three-year-old shouting questions across a crowded restaurant.

As life gets more complex, values become essential. This might be one of the most surprising discoveries we've made over the years: What started as a seemingly pointless exercise has grown increasingly valuable with each passing year and each new responsibility.

Each day brings so many choices about what to do with your time and how to raise your children. You just have to say yes and no to so many more things—soccer or T-ball? Day care or nannies? The routine decisions that seemed simple as individuals or even as a couple become exponentially more complicated when children enter the picture. Each opportunity sounds wonderful in isolation, but collectively they can chip away at core values like togetherness if we're not careful.

Consider how having clarity around values transforms your schedule. For us, knowing that togetherness ranks high among our values has led to creating practical boundaries in our weekly rhythm: one night reserved solely for us as a couple, two or three evenings dedicated to activities with our children, a community dinner night, and the remaining evenings preserved for family dinners at home.

These are intentional allocations of our most precious resource (time) guided by our most precious compass (values). The beauty is that when friends invite us to a double date or an exciting event that conflicts with our family night, we don't agonize over the decision or succumb to FOMO. The answer becomes clear because we know what truly matters most to us.

I f you're ready to move from theory to practice, here are some approaches that have worked for us over the years (and saved us from countless awkward dinner-party conversations where we pretended to care about things we absolutely didn't):

- PAY ATTENTION TO YOUR FRUSTRATIONS. Notice what consistently bothers you—these irritations often point to values you hold dear. When Andrew found himself annoyed by teammates who didn't ask questions during film sessions or showed no interest in understanding the bigger picture of a play, it revealed how deeply he valued curiosity and a hunger to learn. Your pet peeves aren't just random quirks; they're your values system sending up flares about what matters to you.

- OBSERVE WHAT YOU CELEBRATE. When our son boldly asked strangers their names in the restaurant, we felt pride rather than embarrassment. This positive reaction signaled our genuine value of curiosity, rather than something we claimed to appreciate on our vision board. Notice what makes you beam with pride versus what makes you cringe— both reactions are valuable data.

- LOOK FOR PATTERNS IN YOUR DECISIONS. Review the major choices you've made in your life. What consistent themes emerge? If you've repeatedly chosen roles that offer autonomy over those promising higher status, independence might be a core value for you. If you keep gravitating toward jobs with flexible schedules despite the pay cuts, maybe work-life balance isn't just a buzzword for you; it's a core operating principle.

- NOTICE WHERE YOU SPEND DISCRETIONARY TIME AND MONEY. These resources flow toward what we truly value, rather than what we claim to value. Your bank statement and calendar reveal truths about your priorities that mere words might obscure. If you say family is your top priority but your credit card statement suggests you're financing a small art supply store, maybe creativity deserves a spot on your official values list.

- CONSIDER WHAT YOU WANT TO PASS ON. Think about what qualities or principles you most want your children, mentees, or those who look up to you to embody. These often reflect your deepest values. What would you want written about you in a eulogy? (Morbid but effective—nothing clarifies values like imagining what you'd want people to remember about you.)

Don't be discouraged if your first attempt feels contrived or if your initial list looks different after six months. Our understanding of our own values has evolved significantly over time—from a five-minute exercise that felt like homework to an hour-long discussion to eventually a three-day intensive process that we actually look forward to (yes, we've become those people who get excited about values-clarification retreats).

Once you've identified your values, make them visible. Write them somewhere you'll see regularly. Discuss them with your partner or close friends—the people who will lovingly call you out when your actions drift from your stated values. Create traditions that celebrate them. The more present they are in your consciousness, the more effectively they'll guide your commitments.

This is what values give you: a filter. The world has endless opinions about what should matter—your morning routine, your network, your kid's preschool. But when you've done the work to know what actually matters to you, the noise fades.

You stop chasing what's good and start choosing what's right. That's the difference between depletion and purpose. Between a life that looks impressive and one that feels like yours.

VALUES WORK LIKE BOUNCERS. They stand at the door of your life, deciding which opportunities get in and which ones wait outside. Most filtering happens automatically.

YOUR FRUSTRATIONS ARE CLUES. What consistently bothers you points to principles you hold dear. Annoyance at teammates not maximizing talent reveals you value diligence. Irritation at inefficiency means you prize effectiveness.

YOUR SPENDING TELLS THE TRUTH. Bank statements and calendars are more honest than vision boards. If you claim family is everything but your credit card suggests you're financing an art supply store, creativity deserves official recognition.

VALUES CLARIFY DECISIONS INSTANTLY. When filtered through a core value like "togetherness," seemingly attractive opportunities become obviously wrong choices. Decision paralysis dissolves.

CHILDREN ABSORB VALUES THROUGH WATCHING. A three-year-old shouting questions at strangers in restaurants reflects genuine family curiosity more authentically than any lecture could teach.

VALUES EVOLVE FROM GENERIC TO SPECIFIC. "Honesty" and "respect" eventually become personalized principles like "playfulness" and "generous stewardship" that actually guide real decisions.

8

Love

In this chapter, we want to tackle the "what" question that's unique to romantic love: not just what kind of person to commit to, but what commitment itself looks like when you've found someone worth choosing. Previous chapters helped you identify potential commitments based on your interests, values, and inclinations, but love operates differently. You can't really "discover" the right person the same way you might discover a passion for sourdough or recognize a family pattern pointing toward creativity.

Instead, romantic commitment is often about recognizing when you've found someone who makes you want to be the kind of person who commits fully—someone who makes the leap from "keeping your options open" to "choosing this person, with all their flaws and morning breath, every single day" feel like the most natural thing in the world.

We're not here to tell you whom to choose—that's

a decision only you can make. But we can share what we've learned about how commitment transforms from a scary leap into daily practice, and why choosing someone deeply might be one of the most liberating decisions you'll ever make.

Rather than offering generic relationship advice, we're sharing two letters—one from Andrew to his younger self, and one from Shawn to her younger self—about our journey from the initial attraction we felt to the lasting commitment we've built. These letters capture what we wish we had known when we were first navigating the sometimes confusing, often exhilarating, occasionally mortifying path of romantic commitment.

They speak to our fears, to our missteps, and ultimately to what we learned about the transformative power of choosing someone, day after day, and building a life together—even when that life includes arguments about thermostat settings and whose turn it is to deal with the mysterious smell coming from the refrigerator.

Dear Younger Andrew,

You're sitting in your dorm room at Vanderbilt right now, aren't you? Probably surrounded by engineering textbooks, a football playbook, and whatever protein-packed meal

you've cobbled together that somehow meets your macros but tastes like cardboard. You're meticulously planning your future—the NFL career, the businesses you'll start, the goals you'll conquer.

I know there's a whiteboard somewhere in that room with a five-year plan.

What's not on that whiteboard? A relationship that will completely transform your life. I can picture your reaction: a slight eye roll, followed by "I don't have time for that right now." Trust me, I get it. You're focused. Driven. Convinced that relationships are something you'll get to . . . eventually. When the timing is right.

Here's the truth I wish someone had told me: There is no perfect timing when it comes to love. It arrives unexpectedly—in your case, at the Country Music Awards of all places, where you'll meet an Olympic gold medalist named Shawn who will throw all your carefully laid plans into beautiful disarray.

And that's the first lesson I want to share: The best things in life rarely fit into our preconceived schedules. The relationships that matter most often arrive when we're not looking for them, and they challenge us in ways we never anticipated.

When Shawn tells you she's moving to Nashville, your initial reaction will be . . . complicated. There's excitement, sure, but also a jolt of panic. Suddenly, this person who's been at a safe distance—someone you see occasionally when your schedules align—will be living less than a mile away. The relationship will shift from theoretical to very, very real.

You'll even write her an email (yes, an email—very romantic, past Andrew) outlining your "ground rules" for when she moves to town. I still have it, and honestly, it's equal parts endearing and hilarious. You were so concerned with establishing boundaries, with making sure she knew you had friends and a life and couldn't see her every day. You thought you were protecting yourself from what you feared most: vulnerability.

What you didn't understand then—what took years to truly grasp—is that commitment isn't about perfect planning or having all the answers in advance. It's about deciding, again and again, that this person matters enough to figure things out together. It's about recognizing that your life is better with them in it, even when it's messy or inconvenient or scary.

There will be days when commitment feels easy—like when you're cuddled up watching a movie, or celebrating a milestone, or planning your future together. But the real test comes on ordinary Tuesdays when you're both exhausted, or during that first major fight when walking away seems easier than staying, or in those moments when you realize that loving someone means witnessing their flaws up close.

In those moments, remember this: Love isn't just a feeling. It's a decision you make every single day.

When Shawn moves to Nashville, your relationship won't be perfect. In fact, you'll both make plenty of mistakes. You'll take each other for granted sometimes. You'll struggle to communicate. You'll wrestle with your own independence—that stubborn streak that makes you think you can handle everything on your own.

After you get married, you'll have a tough first year—harder than you expected. You'll both be pursuing careers, often in different cities. You'll miss the excitement of dating and courtship, and you'll mistakenly think that being married means the work is done. It isn't. In many ways, it's just beginning.

The turning point will come about eighteen months in. Life will throw something unexpected your way, and suddenly, all those surface-level frustrations will shrink to their actual size. You'll see her clearly for the first time: your partner in navigating whatever comes. And in that clarity, you'll recommit in a deeper way.

You'll learn that commitment is waking up every morning and choosing this person again. It's picking up the phone when they call, even when you're busy. It's prioritizing family dinners and date nights. It's working through conflict. It's seeing their beautiful qualities and their uniquely terrible traits, and loving them anyway.

And here's what will surprise you: Commitment feels like freedom. The energy you spent wondering what-if becomes energy for building something real. Knowing you're in this for the long haul gives you courage to show up fully—even the messy, unfinished parts of you.

Years from now, you'll look back at the whiteboard in your dorm room and laugh at how narrowly you defined success. Because while achievements matter, what brings real fulfillment is having someone witness your life—someone in the front-row seat, experiencing it all alongside you. Someone who sees you fail and still believes in you. Someone who challenges you to grow but loves you exactly as you are.

So my advice to you, younger Andrew, is simple: When love comes knocking, don't overthink it. Don't try to fit it perfectly into your schedule or manage it with elaborate ground rules. Instead, be brave enough to let it change you. Be willing to adjust your plans. Be open to the possibility that the most meaningful part of your life might be the relationship you haven't even imagined yet.

And when Shawn moves to Nashville, when you're faced with the decision to fully commit or have a "just in case" back-up plan—choose commitment. It won't always be easy, but I promise you this: It will be worth it.

> Your future self,
> Andrew

P.S. You'll still be terrible at texting back. Work on that, will you?

Dear Younger Shawn,

You're sitting in a hotel room somewhere between competitions, aren't you? Suitcase half unpacked because there's no point when you'll be leaving again in a day or two. Your entire life fits into that suitcase now—competition credentials from cities you barely remember, leotards covered with chalk, and just enough normal clothes to remind you that somewhere, a regular teenage life exists. But not for you.

You've learned to be self-sufficient in ways most people twice your age haven't mastered. You've traveled the world, stood on Olympic podiums, felt the weight of a nation's expectations on your shoulders. And somewhere along the way, you've convinced yourself that independence equals strength, that needing others is a weakness you can't afford.

I'm writing to tell you something you won't believe right now: The bravest thing you'll ever do isn't a balance beam routine in Beijing. It's opening your heart to someone else.

One day, you'll meet a football player. He'll be tall, thoughtful, and unexpectedly kind. You'll exchange numbers, thinking it's just another fleeting connection in your whirlwind life. You won't realize it then, but this moment will change everything.

You've spent your entire life in control—mastering routines, perfecting dismounts, calculating risks. Relationships don't work that way. They're messy and unpredictable. They require different kinds of courage: the courage to be vulnerable, to let someone see behind the smile you've perfected for cameras, and the courage to commit to a person, not an outcome. To stay, to show up, to be seen.

When you start falling for Andrew, it will terrify you. Your instinct will be to keep him at a distance—dating long-distance feels safe because it allows you to compartmentalize. You can be "Shawn the girlfriend" on weekends, then return to being independent Shawn the rest of the time. No need to fully integrate these parts of yourself.

Then will come the decision that scares you most: moving to Nashville. On the surface, you'll tell yourself (and him) that you're not moving there for him. You're doing it for yourself, for your career, for a change of scenery. And while that's partly true, let's be honest with each other now: You're moving there because something inside you recognizes that what you have with Andrew deserves a real chance.

You'll send him an email before the move, pouring out your anxieties about this step. About how fiercely independent you are. About how you've built walls to protect yourself from depending on anyone. About how previous relationships taught you that no matter how invested you are, the other person might not reciprocate. Your words will reveal the core fear you've never articulated: that you're "unlovable" if someone gets too close.

Let me tell you something important: That fear is normal, but it isn't true.

The move to Nashville will feel like jumping without knowing if there's a net below. You'll rent an extended-stay hotel room first, hesitant to fully commit. But with each day, each dinner shared, each ordinary moment of just being together, something will shift. You'll realize that commitment expands you into a fuller version of yourself.

There will be challenges, of course. The transition from Olympic athlete to non-athlete is jarring enough without adding relationship navigation to the mix. You'll struggle with your identity, with finding purpose beyond competition. There will be days when you wonder if you made a mistake, if you should have stayed in the familiar comfort of Des Moines surrounded by family.

But when you first have a child together, you'll watch Andrew become a father and see commitment take on an entirely new dimension. The same man who once wrote formal emails about "ground rules" will get up at 3 a.m. for feedings without complaint, will rearrange his entire schedule around nap time, will somehow make diaper changes look like an Olympic sport he's determined to medal in.

You'll realize that commitment is about building a family, creating traditions, becoming the kind of people who show up for each other through sleepless nights and tantrum-filled afternoons. The independence you treasured was a smaller, lonelier version of life.

Over time, you'll discover something paradoxical: True independence comes through interdependence. Being strong means having the courage to let someone help carry your burdens. It means creating space for another person in your meticulously controlled life and finding that the messiness they bring is actually beautiful.

The girl who lived out of a suitcase will put down roots. The athlete who thrived on perfection will learn to embrace imperfection. The independent spirit who feared vulnerability will discover that being known—truly, deeply known—is the greatest gift of all.

So as you sit in that hotel room, wondering if there's more to life than medals and expectations, know this: There is. There's a love story waiting for you that will challenge everything you think you know about strength and independence. There's a partner who will see past the Olympic gold medalist to the person underneath—who will love your accomplishments but also your quirks, your flaws, your humanity.

With all my love,
Your future self

P.S. When Andrew sends you that adorably formal email about "ground rules" for when you move to Nashville, save it. Years later, you'll both laugh about it, and it will remind you how far you've come.

LOVE IS BOTH FEELING AND CHOICE—BUT CHOICE CARRIES THE DAY. The butterflies of early romance can carry a relationship only so far; eventually, desire must transform into the daily decision to show up, prioritize, and choose this person again.

PERFECT TIMING IS A MYTH. The best relationships often arrive when we're not looking for them, disrupting our carefully laid plans and forcing us to choose between our schedules and our hearts.

COMMITMENT BECOMES FREEDOM. By choosing one person and closing other doors, you gain the space to build something deep and lasting.

VULNERABILITY IS THE BRAVEST ACT. For high achievers accustomed to independence and control, letting someone witness your failures, quirks, and 3 a.m. anxieties requires more courage than any public performance.

MARRIAGE IS THE STARTING LINE. The real work begins after "I do"—learning

to communicate, prioritizing each other
through busy seasons, and choosing
connection over convenience day
after day.

GROUND RULES REVEAL OUR FEARS.
Those early attempts to manage and
control new love (like Andrew's formal
email about boundaries) often mask
our deepest terror: that we might not be
lovable if someone gets too close.

9

The Unknown

In Homer's **Odyssey**, the hero, Odysseus, faces a daunting challenge: navigating his ship past the island of the Sirens, whose irresistible song lures sailors to their doom. Odysseus knows he must pass the island to return home to his family. Turning back isn't an option. So he devises an audacious plan: He instructs his men to tie him to the mast so he can hear the legendary song without acting on its deadly allure. He has no idea if it will work.

We face our own version of this constantly, though usually with less rope and fewer mythical creatures. We're asked to commit to people, projects, and paths while standing at the threshold of the unknown. Should I pursue this relationship? Start this business? Move to a new city, learn this skill, follow this dream—all without any guarantee of the outcome?

The modern response to uncertainty is to remain uncommitted. Keep options open. Maintain backup plans. Avoid tying yourself to the mast of any single choice. If we don't know what lies ahead, isn't it wiser to preserve our freedom to pivot?

This logic overlooks something fundamental: The most profound rewards in life come through commitment, especially commitment made in the face of the unknown. The best relationships, the most meaningful work, the deepest growth—they all require venturing into uncharted territory.

What we've discovered is that sometimes you need to commit before knowing if something is "your thing." Love and enjoyment often grow from the seeds of commitment, even when initial feelings are lukewarm. Ready is a decision, not a feeling. You may never feel it. Decide anyway.

I'll admit—when I first RSVP'd "yes" to a women's Bible study group, it was more out of a sense of duty than any burning passion to study scripture. That first meeting went fine, but it was more awkward small talk than soul-stirring inspiration. The group seemed pleasant enough, but too earnest for my taste.

About six or seven meetings in, I started distancing myself from the group. Life got busy and those study sessions kept getting deprioritized. Chores to do, work deadlines to push. The group kept trucking along fine without me. Until, at the tenth meeting—the one I had decided would be my last—one of the faithful attendees decided to call me out on my wishy-washy presence.

She did it so gracefully, pointing out that she and others noticed my absence and that my contributions were missed. Her comment made me feel like I mattered to this group. It also caught me off guard in the best possible way. Her words sparked something in me: I realized that these women had shown up for me, and that maybe it was time I actually invested in showing up for them.

So I recommitted—I planted my feet back in that circle and attended the meetings with focused conviction. And then, in a plot twist that no one saw coming, the entire group dissolved a few weeks later.

It broke up for logistical reasons—people moving to different parts of the city, babies on the way—nothing contentious or dramatic. But I felt a strange sense of betrayal. Here I was, finally ready to open up and be vulnerable, and suddenly the opportunity vanished. It was like working up the courage to jump into a pool only to find it had been drained while my eyes were closed.

In that moment, I could easily have told myself, "See? This is exactly why I don't commit to things like this." It would have confirmed all my initial reservations about making deep connections. But something unexpected happened instead. That brief glimpse of authentic community—even if it had slipped through my fingers—had revealed a hunger in me that I couldn't ignore.

What came next was harder than anything I'd done before. I had to reach out to women I wasn't particularly close with and essentially say, "Hey, I want us to be real friends." As an only child who had spent much of my life bouncing from one surface-level connection to another, this felt terrifying. I stared at that draft text for weeks, writing and rewriting, second-guessing myself at every turn.

You see, being in the public eye from the age of twelve taught me a peculiar lesson: People were interested in my achievements, my medals, my performances, but rarely in just me. I became comfortable with a certain kind of distance, a protective barrier between myself and others. I could host the Bible study in my home, provide snacks, facilitate discussion, all without ever truly opening myself to being known.

But that one gentle confrontation—"I want more from you"—pierced something in me. It was the first time in my adult life someone had essentially said: Your presence matters more than your performance.

So I sent that terrifying text. And another. And

another. I initiated a new group, but this time with clear expectations from the beginning: We would be vulnerable, we would support each other, we would commit to showing up authentically and consistently.

The group that formed from those hesitant invitations has become my true support system. We text every day. We show up for each other in ways I never imagined possible. They know the real me—not Olympic Shawn or Internet Shawn or any other public version of myself. Just me, with all my doubts and fears and hopes.

What amazes me most is that I couldn't have discovered what I truly needed without first committing to something unknown. Had I waited until I felt certain, I might never have experienced the connection I now cherish.

So many of us wait to feel passionate before we commit—to relationships, communities, causes. We want certainty first. But sometimes the equation works in reverse. Passion is often a byproduct. Commitment shapes what we care about by giving us something to care for.

When I look at my marriage, my business ventures, I see the same pattern. The most meaningful parts of my life are the ones I committed to despite the unknowns. Somewhere along the way, that steady choice grew into something I can't imagine living without.

When I think about commitment in the face of uncertainty, I'm reminded of "orienteering"—the wilderness navigation skill I first encountered as a gangly Boy Scout and later refined during a brief, humbling stint spent training with Special Forces units.

Picture this: You're dropped in unfamiliar woods with nothing but a compass and a wrinkled map. You know your destination, but the path? Not so much. No trail signs, no GPS, no friendly ranger. Just you, your compass, and trees that all look suspiciously alike.

You identify your position, locate your destination, and set a bearing. Then comes the real test: moving forward while paying attention to the world around you. That distinctive hill on the horizon. The unexpected creek that wasn't on the map. Each surprise either confirms you're on course or signals it's time to recalibrate.

The magic of orienteering is having a tool that keeps you moving in roughly the right direction regardless of what emerges. The compass doesn't eliminate the unknown; it gives you a way to move through it.

This is exactly how commitment works. The unknown is the whole point. If we knew with certainty how every commitment would unfold, where would we find growth? Discovery? The blank spaces in the map are where all the good stuff happens.

When Shawn and I started dating, we couldn't have known what lay ahead. She had Olympic gold and could flip across balance beams the width of my thumb. I had football aspirations and a special talent for throwing a ball backward between my legs with pinpoint accuracy. There was no road map for combining our wildly different lives.

But we committed to a direction together, using shared values as our compass. Would her celebrity complicate things? Would my career keep us apart? Yes and yes. We didn't need to predict every challenge. We just needed to know what mattered most to us.

It reminds me of how they train bank tellers to spot counterfeit money. The method is surprisingly simple: Touch, tilt, look at, look through. You learn the specific feel of the cotton-linen paper—slightly rough, with a distinctive texture that cheap copies can't replicate. You memorize where the watermarks sit, how the color-shifting ink changes when you angle the bill toward the light, the exact spot where the security thread glows pink or green under UV light.

Experienced tellers say they can feel a fake before they see it. After handling thousands of genuine bills, their fingers register something "off" about a counterfeit—often a waxy smoothness where texture should be. They don't need to know every counterfeiting technique. They just know the real thing so intimately that anything false announces itself.

That's what shared values did for our relationship. We got clear on what was true for us—what we stood for, what we wouldn't compromise on, what kind of life we wanted to build. When something felt off, we could sense it. When a decision aligned with who we were, we knew. The compass worked because we'd studied it closely enough to trust it.

This applies far beyond relationships. When we commit to learning a skill, starting a business, or pursuing a creative passion, we never have complete information. Instead, we set a direction based on what matters, check our bearings as we go, and let commitment transform aimless wandering into exploration with purpose.

Sometimes there's even an advantage to not knowing what lies ahead. A little naivete can be a gift—if we truly understood how hard some things would be, we might never begin. And maybe that's the point. Commitment was never meant to be a reward for certainty. It's a way of moving through a world that will never offer us certainty. The unknown is the whole reason it matters.

So now that we've tied ourselves to the mast like Odysseus, how do we put this philosophy into practice? How do we commit when the path ahead has all the clarity of a foggy morning, and the GPS of life is stubbornly announcing "recalculating" every five minutes?

Here are some approaches that have worked for us and for countless others who've learned to dance with uncertainty rather than hide from it:

FOCUS ON DIRECTION RATHER THAN DESTINATION

Imagine you're sailing a boat. You can't control the wind or the waves, but you can adjust your sails and choose your bearing. Instead of demanding complete certainty about where you'll dock (spoiler alert: life rarely provides that luxury), focus on whether a commitment moves you in a direction aligned with your deepest values.

Ask yourself: "Is this choice consistent with who I want to become?" rather than "Will this definitely succeed?" The first question you can answer now; the second question sometimes takes years to reveal itself. When Andrew considered leaving the NFL to pursue content creation, he couldn't predict success, but he knew the direction aligned with his values of creativity, connection, and family. That was a compass reading he could trust, even when the destination remained hazy.

EMBRACE THE EXPERIMENTAL MINDSET

The word "commitment" often carries the

weight of forever. But what if we framed new commitments as experiments instead? "I'm going to try this yoga thing for three months" feels infinitely more approachable than "I'm committing to becoming a yoga person for the rest of my natural life."

This experimental framing reduces pressure while still creating space for meaningful engagement. Set a specific time frame—three months, six months, a year—to fully immerse yourself before reevaluating. (And yes, this works for almost everything except having children. That experiment runs considerably longer than six months, as we've discovered.)

Shawn approached our YouTube channel with this mindset: "Let's see if we can pay our mortgage with videos for six months." It allowed us to dive in without the paralyzing pressure of making a lifetime career decision. The time-bound experiment gave us freedom to explore, learn, and ultimately discover a path we couldn't have anticipated.

DESIGN YOUR ENVIRONMENT FOR SUCCESS

Like Odysseus tied to the mast, create an environment that supports your commitment when your future self inevitably starts eyeing the escape hatch. This isn't about tricking yourself; it's about acknowledging that humans are remarkably creative when it comes to sabotaging their own best intentions.

When we decided to prioritize family dinners, we physically moved our phones to a dedicated "phone home" during meals— a small environmental adjustment that dramatically changed our behavior.

Sometimes the most effective commitment device is simply putting something on a calendar. In our household, if it's scheduled, it gains a sacred status that helps it survive the daily chaos. But if it fails to claim territory on the family calendar, it competes with a thousand other priorities and inevitably loses.

LOOK FOR SIGNS RATHER THAN CERTAINTY

Return to our orienteering metaphor: When navigating unfamiliar terrain, you look for landmarks that indicate you're on the right track. You don't need absolute certainty about the entire journey; you just need enough confirmation to take the next step.

These navigational cues might include small moments of enjoyment ("I actually looked forward to practicing today"), signs of progress ("This used to be impossible for me"), or positive feedback from others ("Your writing is starting to flow more naturally"). Each of these "terrain features" provides valuable data about your direction, even when the destination remains obscured by the horizon.

When Shawn started her podcast, she didn't have ironclad proof it would succeed—but the early listener feedback provided enough directional confirmation to keep moving forward, one episode at a time.

It reminds us of an old teaching about the Israelites at the Red Sea. According to tradition, the sea didn't part the moment they arrived. It wasn't until one man stepped into the water, up to his nose, that the sea finally made way. The path didn't appear **before** the step of faith; it appeared **because** of it. Sometimes, that's how commitment works. You move forward into uncertainty, trusting that the ground will rise to meet you—or the sea will split—only once you've taken the first few impossible steps.

MASTER THE ART OF SHOWING UP

Sometimes the most powerful commitment isn't flashy or complicated—it's simply showing up, especially when motivation has gone on vacation and left no forwarding address. The writer who sits at the desk even when inspiration is playing hard to get. The partner who remains engaged even during conversations that would win Olympic medals for awkwardness. The athlete who trains even on days when the couch presents a compelling alternative life philosophy.

This showing-up muscle might be the most important one you'll ever develop. Because here's the truth that Instagram influencers rarely mention: The path to any meaningful achievement is paved with thoroughly unmotivated moments when you showed up anyway.

In our marriage, some of our most significant breakthroughs came on days when neither of us particularly felt like having that difficult conversation, but we showed up for it regardless, because that's what we'd committed to doing.

FIND CLARITY THROUGH MOVEMENT

If you're waiting for perfect clarity before taking action, you might be standing still for a very long time. Instead of trying to think your way to clarity, seek clarity through action. Each step you take in a committed direction reveals new information that helps refine your path.

It's like trying to navigate a dark room. You can stand frozen by the doorway, hoping for the lights to suddenly come on, or you can start moving carefully through the space, using touch to gradually build a mental map of what's around you.

When we launched our first business, we had more questions than answers. But each step—each product created, each customer interaction, each mistake made—illuminated the path forward in ways that no amount of preliminary planning could have achieved. Movement creates momentum, which in turn generates clarity.

FIND YOUR FELLOW TRAVELERS

Finally, commit alongside others when possible. Few things make the unknown more navigable than having companions on the journey. Community provides support (for when you falter), feedback (for when you need new perspectives), and accountability (for when you're tempted to quit), making it easier to traverse uncertain territory.

Think about joining a group dedicated to your commitment, whether it's a writing circle, a fitness class, or a mastermind group for entrepreneurs. On mornings when your motivation is hibernating and your body or mind is staging a protest, knowing others are waiting for you can be the gentle push you need. The shared journey illuminates the path in ways a solo expedition never could, through others' experiences, their encouragement, and their ability to provide perspective when you're too close to your own challenges.

We've experienced this repeatedly—Shawn with her gymnastics teammates, who understood the daily grind of training; Andrew with his football team, where collective commitment elevated individual performance. Even now, we seek out communities for our business ventures, our creative pursuits, and our personal growth. There's profound wisdom in the ancient practice of traveling together, especially when the destination remains partially obscured by the fog of uncertainty.

We began this chapter with Odysseus, bound to the mast by choice, committing to an untested plan while navigating perilous waters toward home. His story reminds us that sometimes the freest choice we can make is to bind ourselves to what matters most, especially when the path ahead remains shrouded in mystery.

In our culture of endless options and instant knowledge, there's something almost rebellious about embracing the unknown. We're expected to research, analyze, and optimize every decision—from which blender to buy to which person to marry. We scroll through reviews, compare features, consult experts. We treat life choices like consumer purchases, demanding certainty before commitment.

The most beautiful commitments often work differently. They're the ones we make before we know how they'll unfold.

We've found this to be true in our own lives. The moments we've leapt without perfect information—starting a business with no entrepreneurial experience, becoming parents without the faintest clue what we were doing, moving across the country on a professional hunch—have yielded our richest rewards. Not because these choices were perfect or painless, but because they created space for discovery that careful planning never could have.

Think about it: The unknown is where all the good stuff lives. Surprise birthday parties. Unexpected friendships. Talents you discover by accident. It's your spouse doing something so tender after fifteen years that it stops you mid-sentence. Your child saying something so insightful it takes your breath away. Capacities within yourself you're still uncovering.

If we eliminated all unknowns before committing, we'd rob ourselves of these discoveries. We'd turn the wild, winding journey of life into a sterile, predictable commute. We'd reduce the magnificent adventure of human connection to something more like a business transaction.

This doesn't mean we throw caution completely to the wind. There's wisdom in gathering information, in testing waters, in seeking counsel. But there's also wisdom in recognizing when it's time to stop researching and start living, when it's time to close the review tabs and take the leap.

Perhaps this is what commitment ultimately asks of us: courage in the face of uncertainty. Perfect attention to what emerges along the way, even when we can't see the full path. The willingness to venture into the unknown for the sake of what we love.

So as you consider your own commitments—to people, to work, to causes, to dreams—we invite you to make friends with the unknown. Because the sea parts after you step in. Not before.

ODYSSEUS TIED HIMSELF TO THE MAST. He committed before knowing if his plan would work. Some of life's most profound rewards require action in the face of uncertainty, not after it's resolved.

THE UNKNOWN IS THE POINT. If we knew exactly how every commitment would unfold, where would we find growth, discovery, or those moments when you surprise yourself by handling the impossible?

PASSION OFTEN FOLLOWS COMMITMENT. Shawn's Bible study experience: What began as lukewarm duty became genuine love through sustained engagement. Feeling can emerge from doing.

NAVIGATE BY COMPASS, NOT MAP. Ask "Is this consistent with who I want to become?" rather than demanding certainty about outcomes. Quicksand wasn't on the map, but north is still north.

MOVEMENT CREATES CLARITY. Instead of waiting for perfect understanding before acting, take steps. Each one reveals new information that helps refine your path.

FRAME COMMITMENTS AS EXPERIMENTS. "Yoga for three months" reduces pressure while creating space for meaningful engagement. Time-bound trials lower the stakes of beginning.

10

Endings

The conversation around commitment often focuses exclusively on perseverance. But sometimes, the most courageous act of commitment is recognizing when a particular path has served its purpose.

The more we reflected on our own experiences—from Olympic gymnastics and NFL careers to business ventures and relationships—the more we realized that understanding how and when to end commitments is essential to cultivating a life of meaningful dedication. Without this wisdom, commitment can degrade into blind stubbornness, tying us to paths that no longer align with our deepest values or serve our highest good.

The question is what to commit to, and for how long. The bar for walking away from central commitments—marriage, family—is rightfully higher than for peripheral ones like hobbies or short-term projects. But all endings require thoughtfulness, integrity, and courage.

In this chapter, we'll explore how to navigate the complex terrain of concluding commitments with grace and purpose. We'll share our experiences of endings both painful and liberating, and offer frameworks for discerning when a commitment has run its course. Most importantly, we'll discuss how to approach endings as natural transitions that honor the time and energy we've invested while creating space for new growth and deeper alignment with who we were made to be.

It's tempting to see only two options: all in or quitter. The healthiest endings we've lived through are more interesting than that. They're thoughtful, earned through genuine discernment, and they usually share several key elements:

EXHAUSTING THE OPTIONS FOR RENEWAL

Before walking away from significant commitments, especially those central to our identity or relationships, it's important to explore every avenue for revitalization. This might mean seeking outside perspective, trying new approaches, or temporarily stepping back to gain clarity.

As Shawn discovered with gymnastics, sometimes simply taking a short break can help reconnect with the foundational love that sparked the commitment in the first place. When she felt overwhelmed by the intensity of Olympic-level training, her coach and parents wisely suggested she take a few days off. During those breaks, she found herself missing "just going to the gym and flipping around for pure enjoyment," and reconnecting with the childlike passion that had first drawn her to the sport.

RECOGNIZING DIMINISHING RETURNS

Every commitment follows a natural arc of investment and return. In the beginning, our efforts often yield dramatic progress as we build fundamental skills and understanding. Over time, continued investment may produce smaller incremental gains. While this isn't necessarily a reason to end a commitment—mastery requires pushing through plateaus—there comes a point when additional investment yields minimal or even negative returns.

For Andrew, this realization came during his NFL career. Despite years of dedication, he found himself still a bubble player, very much on the margin. Meanwhile, his entrepreneurial pursuits were flourishing, offering greater growth and impact for the same investment of time and energy. The contrast made it increasingly clear that continuing to pursue football was costing him opportunities for more meaningful contributions elsewhere.

HONORING EVOLVING PRIORITIES

The commitments that serve us well in one season of life may become misaligned as our circumstances and priorities shift. Rather than clinging to outdated commitments out of inertia or fear, we can acknowledge that what once fit perfectly may no longer serve our highest goals.

Andrew thinks about how, in his twenties, he was deeply loyal to his friends—spending nearly all his free time with them. Then came a girlfriend he could see a serious future with, and his time and loyalty began to shift. Now, as a parent, he spends most of his time on family-oriented activities and far less on hobbies or friends. He cares differently now. Priorities evolve as life does.

When we launched our coffee company, Unicorn Coffee, we poured two years of passion and effort into building something we believed in. The business was gaining traction, with loyal customers who loved our product. But as our family grew and other business opportunities emerged that better aligned with our evolving goals, we began to feel the pressure of shrinking margins—not just financially, but in terms of time, energy, and focus. We realized we couldn't do everything well. Ending the coffee venture was about focusing our limited resources where they could make the most meaningful impact.

LISTENING TO TRUSTED VOICES

Deep investment clouds perspective. That's why we need people who know us well, care about us, and can still see us clearly.

When Andrew was wrestling with his NFL future, a trusted mentor spotted patterns Andrew couldn't see himself. That's the gift of outside counsel: someone who loves you enough to pay attention but stands far enough back to see the whole picture. They catch the disconnect between your stated priorities and where your energy actually goes.

On the surface, ending a commitment might seem like the opposite of commitment—the commitment equivalent of ordering a diet soda with your extra-large fries. But viewed through a wider lens, strategic endings often serve our deeper commitments by allowing us to reallocate our most precious resources: time, energy, and attention.

Take our ill-fated subscription box business. Years ago, I found myself upstairs in our home office, doing a victory dance after thousands of sign-ups poured in for our new venture. I bounded downstairs to share the exciting news with Shawn, already imagining the thriving business we were about to build. "Honey, we're going to be the next Birchbox—but for athletes!"

There was just one tiny problem. In my entrepreneurial enthusiasm, I'd skipped a few minor details—like securing contracts with suppliers, telling Shawn, or figuring out how we'd actually fulfill all these orders while I was busy getting tackled by three-hundred-pound linemen in my day job with the NFL.

In my mind, these were mere technicalities. "Look at all this collateral we have now!" I argued, waving printouts of our sign-up numbers. "We can shop better deals with suppliers! We basically have start-up capital! We'll hire a team! This is happening!"

Shawn, being the voice of reason in our marriage (a full-time job in itself), looked at me with that expression I've come to know well: a mix of loving patience and "bless your heart" concern. "We don't have time for this," she said calmly. "We don't have the structure. We don't have the logistics figured out." She was protecting commitments that actually mattered—our family, my existing career obligations, dreams that were already reality.

Refunding everyone's money was humbling. In the age of social media, where everyone's an armchair CEO ready to critique your every move, admitting defeat before we'd shipped a single box stung. But spreading ourselves thinner than tissue paper would have been worse. By ending one commitment, we preserved our ability to invest fully in others.

This pattern has repeated across our lives. When Shawn retired from gymnastics, she still loved the sport. She could have continued, but she recognized that the resources required to remain elite would crowd out aspirations that had become more important.

Similarly, my decision to stop participating in NFL tryouts came only after years of dedication and honoring my past investments. While I had achieved my core dream of playing in the NFL, the continuous cycle of being signed, cut, and called back for tryouts felt less like the productive friction that builds strength and more like a destructive pattern that diminishes identity.

I was trying to serve two masters—and football had become the one pulling me away from my real future. My heart was increasingly drawn to building businesses and learning about media— pursuits that fed my value of constant learning and curiosity. I recognized that committing to the next great version of myself—the entrepreneur and creator—required reallocating the finite well of attention and energy that the NFL cycle consumed. The commitment was redeemed by applying the competitive spirit and discipline built through football toward pursuits that could scale beyond what a football career could offer.

The truth is that our capacity for meaningful commitment isn't infinite. Every significant commitment draws from the same well of attention and energy. It's like trying to stream Netflix, download updates, and video chat simultaneously on hotel Wi-Fi—something's got to buffer.

Even when endings make perfect rational sense, they rarely feel simple emotionally. Concluding a significant commitment—whether it's a career, relationship, business venture, or community role—often triggers a complex mix of feelings: loss, failure, relief, shame, and uncertainty. Acknowledging and navigating this emotional terrain is essential for ending commitments with integrity and grace.

When we finally decided to end Andrew's pursuit of an NFL career, the ripple effects extended far beyond our personal experience. The whole unraveling process continued for weeks and months afterward in unexpected ways. He'd bump into acquaintances at the grocery store, who'd casually ask if he was still playing. Former teammates would text, assuming he was still in the game. People continued associating him so closely with football that his identity and the sport seemed inseparable in their minds.

These interactions created moments of awkwardness and sometimes genuine pain. We remember him showing up at Thanksgiving dinner where family members excitedly asked about football—what team might call next, whom he was training with, when the next tryout would be. The moment he shared that he was done playing, an uncomfortable silence would follow. In those pauses, we realized that football was the primary way they related to him. Without it, some weren't sure what else to discuss.

Shawn experienced similar emotional complexity when her Bible study group dissolved just after she had finally committed to being vulnerable and fully engaged. She felt betrayed initially, having just taken the emotional risk to invest more deeply. In her mind, she had made an internal switch to share vulnerabilities and build closer connections, envisioning a friend group she could be part of long-term. The timing of the group's dissolution following her decision to engage more authentically felt particularly painful.

These emotional responses—betrayal, embarrassment, sadness, uncertainty—are natural parts of the ending process. Rather than trying to bypass them or pretend they don't exist, we've found several approaches helpful in navigating this terrain:

ACKNOWLEDGE THE GRIEF

Even endings that are clearly right can involve genuine loss. Giving ourselves permission to feel sad about what we're leaving behind honors the significance that the commitment held in our lives. When Andrew stepped away from football, allowing himself to grieve the camaraderie, the structure, and even the identity it provided was crucial for moving forward healthily.

SEEK CLOSURE

After her Bible study group dissolved, Shawn made a point of communicating individually with each person, making sure that the ending wasn't about her or something she had done wrong. This was about creating emotional clarity that allowed her to move forward. By addressing lingering questions and concerns, she created space for whatever might come next.

REFRAME THE NARRATIVE

How we tell the story of our endings shapes how we and others experience them. When our subscription box venture failed to launch successfully, we were surprised by the predominantly positive feedback from potential customers. Most people expressed understanding and assured us they'd support future ventures. This supportive response created constructive pressure—we felt obligated to live up to their belief in us by creating something worthy of their continued support.

FIND THE LESSONS

Every ending, especially difficult ones, contains valuable wisdom if we're willing to look for it. When Andrew was cut from the Chiefs, his coach offered a perspective that initially stung, but proved invaluable: He had the talent to play in the NFL but needed to develop a more professional approach. That feedback shaped our approach to future commitments both in and beyond sports, helping us understand the difference between talent and professional discipline.

The emotional work of endings is about integrating the experience into our journey in a way that leads to growth. Even painful endings can become fertile soil. And the emotions that accompany them are signals guiding us toward commitments that fit better and a deeper understanding of ourselves.

After Shawn's first Bible study group dissolved, she could have concluded that vulnerable community wasn't worth the risk, that putting herself out there was just an invitation for disappointment, like trying to make dinner plans with flaky friends. Instead, she recognized that the taste of connection she'd experienced, however brief, represented something she truly valued.

Even though that initial group didn't work out, she had glimpsed something she genuinely wanted to commit to. More than that, she gained clarity about what it would take to make it work next time, including what she herself needed to do differently.

This realization led her to consider how she might create that connection herself, rather than waiting for the perfect group to magically appear.

This perspective inspired her to form a new group with clearer intentions from the very beginning. They even took the time to explicitly write down what they wanted the group to be—expectations around vulnerability, consistency, and mutual support. Because of this shared understanding, they bonded more quickly, and the group has endured where the previous one dissolved.

What might have seemed like failure became the foundation for something more authentic and enduring. The ending created necessary space for a beginning that better aligned with her deepest values and needs. Think of it like finally admitting that your current workout routine isn't working (we see you, unused gym membership) and finding an activity you actually enjoy instead of one you think you should enjoy.

This pattern repeats throughout our lives with surprising regularity. When we left our coffee business behind, it freed us to focus on projects with greater impact and reach. When Andrew concluded his NFL journey, he could focus more fully on building businesses.

The key is approaching endings as strategic reallocations of our most precious resources. Every hour, every ounce of emotional energy, every bit of creative capacity we invest is a choice—about what we're saying yes to, but also what we're saying no to by default.

This doesn't mean we should quit at the first sign of difficulty—we're certainly not advocating for abandoning projects the moment they require actual effort. But there's wisdom in recognizing when persistence has crossed the line into stubbornness, when loyalty has become inertia, when what once served us well has become a beautiful prison of our own making.

When we approach endings this way—with intention rather than impulse, with gratitude rather than guilt—these conclusions become transitions. They're natural passages in an ongoing journey, crafting a life rich in meaning and aligned with who we were put here to be. They're like seasonal changes: You need winter to make space for spring, even if winter feels cold and uncomfortable while you're in it.

EXHAUST RENEWAL OPTIONS FIRST.
Try new approaches, seek outside perspective, take temporary breaks. Shawn rediscovered her love for gymnastics by "just flipping around" during gym breaks. Sometimes the spark needs air, not abandonment.

RECOGNIZE DIMINISHING RETURNS.
Every commitment follows an arc: dramatic early progress, then smaller gains, then a point where additional investment produces minimal or negative returns. Know where you are on the curve.

PRIORITIES EVOLVE ACROSS SEASONS. What serves you brilliantly in one chapter may become misaligned as circumstances shift. The coffee business that once excited can become a distraction from family and better opportunities.

FIND TRUSTED VOICES WHO SEE YOUR BLIND SPOTS. When you're too emotionally invested to see clearly, mentors and friends can spot the disconnect between your stated priorities and actual energy allocation.

GRIEF ACCOMPANIES SMART ENDINGS. Even absolutely right decisions involve genuine loss. Allow yourself to feel sad about what you're leaving behind. False cheerfulness bypasses emotional reality.

ENDINGS CREATE OPENINGS. Strategic conclusions free limited resources for commitments that truly deserve your time, energy, and creative capacity. Walking away wisely is its own form of courage.

How

So here's where things get real.

You've discovered what commitment can do for you—the calm, the joy, the depth, the mastery, the meaning. You've figured out what deserves your devotion, aligned your choices with your deepest values, and maybe even written some heartfelt letters to your younger self about love. You've learned to dance with uncertainty and make strategic endings when necessary.

But now comes the part that separates the dreamers from the doers: actually sustaining your commitments when the initial excitement wears off and real life sets in.

This is where most people stumble. It's easy to commit to something when you're fired up and motivated, when the gym membership is shiny and new, when the relationship feels like a romantic comedy, when the business idea seems like the next billion-dollar unicorn. It's significantly harder to stay committed on Tuesday morning when your alarm goes off in the dark, your motivation has gone missing, and that thing you were so excited about now feels about as appealing as assembling IKEA furniture while hungover.

The next eight chapters aren't about grand gestures or inspirational moments. They're about the unglamorous, essential work of showing up consistently—the infrastructure of commitment that turns good intentions into lasting change. Think of it as the difference between planning an epic road trip and actually doing the maintenance that keeps your car running for the entire journey.

We'll explore how to navigate the inevitable boredom that comes with long-term commitment. How to go public with your commitments in ways that create helpful accountability without turning you into that person who won't stop talking about their new diet. How to design environments that support your commitments instead of sabotaging them. How to find mentors who can guide you through the challenges you haven't even encountered yet.

We'll also tackle the metrics that actually matter, the role of faith when the path gets unclear, why starting over is usually more expensive than sticking it out, and perhaps most importantly, embracing progress over perfection without giving yourself permission to slack off entirely.

This isn't about becoming a commitment robot who never struggles or doubts. It's about building the systems, relationships, and mindsets that help you stay the course when commitment gets hard—which, if you're doing it right, it definitely will.

Ready to learn how to stick with the things that matter? Let's get practical.

11

Boredom

In the corner of a gym in Des Moines, a thirteen-year-old girl falls off the balance beam. Again. For the seventeenth time that day. No crowd cheers. No medals await. Just the hollow echo of another thud, another grunt, another reset. Four hours later, she'll do it again. And the next day. And for thousands of tomorrows after that, until her coach starts to wonder if she's secretly part cat, given her apparent nine lives.

Fast-forward a few years: Millions watch as that same girl—now an Olympic champion—nails a gravity-defying double-twisting double back, making the impossible look effortless. The crowd roars. The commentators gush about natural talent. Someone's grandmother probably tears up a little while eating popcorn on her couch.

But they didn't see the boring parts.

Let's start with the dirty secret of all great achievements: They're built on a foundation of mind-numbing boredom. The specific, repetitive monotony that comes from doing the same thing over and over until your muscle memory could probably do it while you're asleep.

In our culture of productivity hacks, thirty-day challenges, and articles touting "10 Secrets of Overnight Success" (usually written by people whose biggest success was getting a few likes on LinkedIn), admitting this feels almost taboo. We're supposed to stay motivated by switching things up, finding our passion, and riding waves of inspiration.

Here's what no one tells you: Those waves eventually flatten into a still, monotonous sea that stretches to the horizon. And that's where the real journey begins—not on the mountaintop of motivation, but in the valley of "ugh, this again?"

Think of the most exhilarating sports highlight you've ever seen. Then consider what's behind it. The basketball player who hits the game-winning three-pointer? She's shot that exact shot so many times that her body knows the motion better than her conscious mind knows her social security number. The novelist whose twist ending leaves you breathless? He's rewritten those pages until the delete key showed signs of wear.

This chapter is about befriending boredom, because the monotonous middle of any worthwhile pursuit is the system working as designed. And the difference between dabbling and mastery often comes down to something unglamorous: who can tolerate doing the same thing again and again, until excellence becomes inevitable.

I wish I could give you some Olympic champion secret or a neat hack that makes consistency easy. That would be a lie.

The truth? I spent roughly 16,250 hours of my childhood doing the same drills over and over until my hands were calloused and my brain went numb. Of those thousands of hours, maybe 108 were spent in actual competitions—about 0.66 percent. My entire Olympic experience? Sixteen hours total. The balance beam is four inches wide, and I fell off it approximately eight million times before I stuck that Olympic routine.

We live in a world obsessed with shortcuts, with biohacks and productivity apps and morning routines that promise extraordinary results with ordinary effort. But I've watched hundreds of talented gymnasts come and go, and I'll tell you something: The most naturally gifted weren't always the ones who made it. The Olympic team often ended up with the last person standing, the one who could handle showing up when it wasn't exciting anymore.

When her body screamed for a break. When the beam felt like a medieval torture device designed specifically to humble teenage girls.

When I tried coming back for my second Olympics, I was no longer the fresh-faced sixteen-year-old chasing her dreams. I was fighting an eating disorder, recovering from reconstructive surgery, and battling the creeping feeling that my body had given everything it had to give. The boredom was deeper this time—a heavy, existential boredom that questioned why I was even doing this when I could be living a normal life.

What saved me was systems. When my trainer showed up at 5 a.m., I had no choice but to work out. When I broke down the 672 days to Olympic Trials into monthly chunks, the mountain became something I could climb one week at a time.

Think of boredom as a filter that separates the committed from the curious. Anyone can start something when it's shiny and new. Few can navigate the desert of sameness that lies between beginning and mastery, that vast middle where progress happens so slowly you need a microscope to see it.

So here's my advice: Design your life so that showing up requires less willpower than backing out. A 2021 study from USC found that the biggest predictor of lasting habit formation was consistent repetition in the early stages. The people who stuck with their goals were the ones who simply showed up the most in the beginning. Even five minutes a day builds momentum. Consistency is what builds staying power.

Remove the brownies from your pantry. Hire a trainer who expects you and will text you with passive-aggressive concern when you don't show. Make your commitments expensive to break—financially, socially, emotionally. And learn to find small wins in the monotony. My coach taught me to recognize the microscopic improvements that come only through boring repetition. That tiny shift in finger position no one else would notice. That quarter-second longer in the air that felt like nothing but meant everything.

We've experienced this as parents too: When a kid mispronounced a word for weeks, and then slowly, almost imperceptibly, got it right. We didn't see the change happening, but it was. Those unglamorous victories eventually add up to something spectacular: progress that happens in inches, but produces results measurable in miles.

Stick with something long enough, and you realize those small, quiet changes were the good stuff all along.

Boredom, it turns out, is a cognitive feature with evolutionary roots. Our brains are wired to seek novelty, constantly scanning for changes in our environment that might signal opportunity ("Ooh, berries!") or danger ("Ooh, lion!"). When nothing new appears, our dopamine pathways grow restless, our attention wanders, and that siren call of "anything but this" grows louder than a toddler in a library during story time.

What research shows, however, is that the brain's preference for novelty is negotiable. A study on perceived control and boredom found something counterintuitive: We get bored both when we have too much control (the situation lacks challenge) and when we have too little control (we can't effectively engage). The sweet spot lies in the middle—having enough control to feel engaged but enough challenge to stay interested.

Participants who believed they could eventually gain control over a task, even when they currently couldn't, experienced less boredom than those who saw no possibility of improvement. This suggests that the mere prospect of progress, rather than current mastery level, may be what keeps us engaged.

This reveals our first psychological tool for conquering boredom: expectation management. And consider this your heads-up call that great achievements are fundamentally boring—a big reason we wanted to write this book in the first place. When we enter a commitment with clear eyes about the monotonous middle—like acknowledging that learning Spanish will involve more vocabulary flash cards than spontaneous flamenco dancing—we're less likely to interpret that inevitable plateau as failure or reason to quit.

Another key finding comes from flow psychology. We typically associate flow states with excitement, but Mihaly Csikszentmihalyi's research found that many flow experiences begin with pushing through initial boredom. Master craftspeople often report that their most transcendent moments arrive after periods of mechanical repetition—as if boredom itself is a doorway to deeper engagement, not its opposite.

This suggests our second psychological tool: reframing boredom as a signal of approaching mastery rather than a warning to stop. When you feel bored practicing scales on the piano or running your daily route, it might actually indicate that your brain is ready to consolidate skills at a deeper level—or that you've forgotten to change your playlist since 2017 and your brain is staging a musical protest.

Cognitive science also illuminates why breaking larger commitments into smaller milestones works so well. Our brains process achievement through what neuroscientists call "prediction error"—the gap between expected rewards and received rewards. Small, frequent victories create positive prediction errors that release dopamine, refreshing motivation even when the larger goal remains distant. This explains why crossing items off a list feels disproportionately satisfying—each small completion hacks our neurochemistry in favor of persistence, like giving your brain a tiny dessert before dinner is ready.

Perhaps most importantly, research on willpower depletion suggests that fighting boredom through sheer determination is about as effective as trying to put out a fire with a squirt gun. Willpower functions less like a muscle to be strengthened and more like your phone battery—limited, draining faster than you expect, and always running out during crucial moments when you most need GPS directions.

The most successful committers design environments that reduce the cognitive load of consistency. The environmental cues Shawn mentioned—removing temptations from your pantry, scheduling unmissable appointments with trainers who enjoy morning cheerfulness way too much, using visual tracking systems—are sophisticated applications of behavioral psychology that outsource willpower to your surroundings, preserving mental bandwidth for the work itself.

The committed life isn't about learning to enjoy boredom—that would be like trying to enjoy paper cuts or Monday morning meetings. It's about understanding boredom's neurological purpose, anticipating its arrival with all the excitement of a tax audit, and building systems that carry you through the motivational valleys until you reach higher ground. In doing so, you transform boredom from commitment's enemy into one of its most valuable signals, a threshold you cross on the way to mastery that the dilettante, too busy chasing the next shiny object, never experiences.

 I remember sitting in the weight room at Vanderbilt, staring at the forty-five-pound plates I was about to load onto the bar for the 1,273rd time. Not that I was counting. Okay, maybe I was counting, possibly with a slightly concerning level of precision.

The point is, I knew exactly what was coming next: the same sets, the same reps, the same burning sensation, and the same coach shouting the same encouragement with the same enthusiasm that somehow never wavered, as if he were powered by an endless supply of motivational batteries.

And I had an epiphany while gripping that cold metal: Everyone around me was pretending.

They were pretending to like it so they could actually work hard. They were putting in genuine effort, sweating through their shirts and grunting like caffeinated lumberjacks. But they were pretending to be surprised by how boring it all was. "Man, another squat day?" they'd groan with theatrical disappointment. "These agility drills again?" As if each repetition was an unexpected plot twist in their athletic journey rather than the utterly predictable chapter it actually was.

The breakthrough came when I accepted that training was supposed to be boring. Games were chaos and adrenaline. Training was repetition and refinement. That gap was the whole point, like the difference between rehearsing a play and opening night. The monotony of one makes the magic of the other possible.

To make the boredom more digestible, I started creating "mini games" and ridiculous scenarios in my head. I declared myself the mayor of "Meathead City," population whoever was currently lifting in my general vicinity. These were my ways of staying mentally engaged when my body was running on autopilot.

Our culture has created this bizarre expectation that everything should be constantly stimulating. We've Netflix-ified our approach to commitment, expecting each day to deliver a new dopamine hit, a fresh episode, a plot twist worthy of a season finale. And when our pursuits inevitably settle into predictable patterns, we think something's gone wrong, as if we've accidentally subscribed to the world's most boring streaming service.

Nothing's gone wrong. You're just finally arriving at the real work.

I used to have this weird shirt ritual in high school. I'd wear the same unwashed training shirt for an entire year of football. By December, it was basically a biohazard—stiff with salt stains, smelling like something archaeologists would carbon-date, and capable of standing up on its own like a fabric scarecrow. But putting it on was like putting on an identity: This is who I am and what I do, regardless of how I feel about it today.

That crusty yellow shirt was a physical reminder that showing up wasn't optional. It marked the path I was on: toward something I cared about enough to keep going, even when it wasn't glamorous. I wasn't debating whether to train each day. I was just doing the next rep, putting one foot in front of the other, regardless of how inspired I felt.

This is what separates the elite from the merely talented: the ability to make peace with boredom. To recognize that the flatline feeling of "here we go again" is the price of admission to places most people never reach.

I think about my NFL journey and how many guys with more natural talent never made it. Before I got released by the Chiefs, I understood this; I could embrace the boredom, do the unglamorous work day after day. But that rejection disoriented me. As a coping mechanism, I started hedging— pursuing other interests, keeping my options open, telling myself it was smart and ambitious. Really, it was a defense against getting hurt again. And it undermined everything.

What brought me back was remembering how to build the right relationship with the mundane. Motivation doesn't arrive like room service. Commitment doesn't always feel like passion. I knew this. I had just forgotten.

So I relearned how to show up, rain or shine, clean shirt or biohazard. Mastery is built on unglamorous repetition and the stubborn refusal to quit when it stops being fun. So if you're bored with your commitment right now—congratulations. You've arrived at the real starting line. Everyone else got distracted at the registration table, probably by the free T-shirts or the promise of instant transformation. The medal isn't for enjoying every minute of the race; it's for finishing it when most people couldn't stomach the middle miles where nothing exciting happens except the steady accumulation of small improvements.

The first step isn't learning to love the boredom. It's just admitting you're going to be bored, accepting it as the expected terrain, and packing your bags accordingly (maybe include some entertainment for your brain, like becoming the mayor of your own imaginary city). The path to extraordinary almost always runs through long stretches of ordinary. The sooner you make peace with that reality, the sooner you can get on with the business of becoming exceptional.

Shawn spent 16,250 hours falling off that balance beam. But there came a point where she stopped counting falls and started feeling microadjustments in her core, sensing the exact moment her weight shifted. She developed what musicians call "perfect pitch," but for balance. The boredom had transformed into meditative absorption—what outsiders mistake for suffering.

Andrew's crusty yellow shirt marked that same threshold. When you've made the decision to show up so many times it becomes automatic, you free up mental bandwidth for a different kind of engagement. You become the thing itself.

Think about surgeons. After a thousand operations, they've developed something valuable: a relationship with precision itself. Their boredom has evolved into surgical meditation, where the repetitive becomes revelatory. Or consider parents. Changing the 847th diaper, you develop an almost supernatural ability to read your child's needs, to sense shifts in mood and health invisible to others. The boring parts become a master class in human attunement.

This is boredom's secret gift: It clears away the noise of novelty- seeking and lets you develop genuine expertise in presence. When you're no longer chasing what's interesting, you can finally notice what's working. Something shifts in the quality of your attention. You stop watching the clock and start watching the work. In sports, there's a concept called the "quiet eye": the ability to hold your gaze on a target—a basketball hoop, a golf ball, a receiver's hands—for just a fraction of a second longer than feels natural. That barely perceptible pause separates good from great.

The people who build something lasting develop their own version of this. A quiet eye for life. The capacity to hold their attention on what matters when everything else screams for distraction. To see past the tedium of Tuesday to the thing they're actually building.

This is what all those hours are really about— not just accumulating skill but training a quality of attention. Shawn found it on the beam, in the thousand repetitions that stopped feeling like progress and started feeling like presence. Andrew found it under the bar, in the snaps that became meditation. Boredom, fully embraced, becomes a doorway. The repetitive becomes infinite.

The boring part is the curriculum. And if you're lucky enough to be bored by something you once loved, you're not at the end. You may finally be at the beginning of the real thing.

THE MATH IS HUMBLING. Of Shawn's 16,250 training hours, only less than a fraction of 1 percent was spent at the Olympics. The other 99.9 percent was repetitive practice that would never make a highlight reel.

BOREDOM IS A FILTER. It separates the committed from the merely curious, weeding out those who can't handle the desert of sameness that stretches between beginning and mastery.

THE GAP CAUSES THE PAIN. Research shows that people warned about boring tasks experience less frustration. Monotony itself isn't the problem. The distance between expectation and reality is.

OUTSOURCE WILLPOWER ENTIRELY. Don't fight boredom with heroic determination. Create environments where showing up requires less energy than backing out.

FLOW HIDES BEHIND TEDIUM. Master craftspeople report that transcendent moments arrive after periods of mechanical repetition. Boredom is the doorway, not the dead end.

THE MIDDLE IS THE CURRICULUM. When you stop watching the clock and start watching the work, boredom teaches presence, precision, and the kind of deep attention that creates mastery.

12

Going Public

I never planned to make a comeback. Truly.

Two years after standing on the Olympic podium in Beijing with a gold medal around my neck, I was firmly settled into my postgymnastics life. No more chalk-dusted palms, no more 5 a.m. alarms that felt like personal attacks on my humanity, no more haunting the gym like it was my second home (and arguably better decorated than my first).

Just normal eighteen-year-old things—like skiing with friends on my birthday. Which is exactly how I ended up with a catastrophically torn knee and reconstructive surgery two years after my Olympic glory, because apparently my body had developed a sense of irony.

There I was, still on crutches, my knee freshly reconstructed and held together by what I assumed was equal parts modern medical ingenuity and prayer, hired to give an inspirational keynote speech to an arena full of middle and high schoolers. The whole event was being televised live, my corporate sponsors from the last Olympics in Beijing were in attendance, and I was supposed to be the picture of post-Olympic success and wisdom.

I delivered my speech from center stage—one woman surrounded by thousands of kids in stadium seating—feeling oddly vulnerable despite having performed routines for millions of viewers. At least on the balance beam I knew what I was supposed to do.

Then came the Q&A.

Most questions were predictable: "What was it like to win gold?" "How many hours did you train?" "Did you miss eating normal food?" (Okay, maybe they didn't ask that last one, but they should have.) But then one kid stood up and asked the question that would change everything: "Are you going to try for the 2012 Olympics? Are you making a comeback?"

The rational answer was glaringly obvious. I hadn't spoken to my coach in two years. My body was still recovering from major surgery. I'd never even contemplated returning to elite gymnastics. The thought had literally never crossed my mind, not even during those 3 a.m. moments when your brain decides to replay every life decision you've ever made. No American gymnast had ever made a second Olympic team after such a long break.

But something else entirely came out of my mouth.

"Yeah," I heard myself say to thousands of people and live television cameras. "I'm going to do it."

The moment the words left my lips, I felt a flutter of panic that had nothing to do with my reconstructed knee and everything to do with my apparently malfunctioning brain. What had I just done?

As I hobbled offstage on my crutches, my sponsor representative looked like she might need medical attention herself—possibly more urgent than my knee had required. "I don't think you understand what you just did," she whispered, her face pale enough to compete with my hospital gown from two months earlier.

Within minutes, my phone exploded with calls—my coach, my parents, reporters, USA Gymnastics officials. Nobody had seen this coming. Least of all me, who was still trying to figure out if my mouth had been temporarily possessed by some overly optimistic spirit.

Looking back, I realize that announcement was my subconscious throwing me a lifeline I didn't even know I needed. I was at my most vulnerable—physically broken, struggling with an eating disorder I rarely discussed, and feeling lost without the structure that gymnastics had always provided. In that moment of public commitment, I'd effectively recruited the entire world to hold me accountable to reorient my entire life.

I couldn't quietly quit in the privacy of my own mind anymore. Now there would be press conferences, training schedules, expectations from people who took notes and published articles. My coach was already calling with plans that sounded both exciting and terrifying. My sponsors were strategizing comeback narratives. The gymnastics federation was making arrangements for someone who, five minutes earlier, hadn't even been on their radar.

That's the thing about declaring your intentions to the world: The world takes you at your word with a seriousness that can be both inspiring and mildly horrifying. For better or worse, I'd just verbally signed a contract with thousands of witnesses, none of whom would forget what I'd promised.

Was it terrifying? Absolutely. I remember thinking, "What have I done?" as I faced the reality of rebuilding my body from scratch, resurrecting skills that had begun to fade like old photographs, and pushing through the mental barriers that come with serious injury and the knowledge that everyone would be watching to see if I could actually pull this off.

But here's what's strange: That spontaneous, public promise became my anchor. On days when my knee screamed in pain and my confidence wavered like a bad Wi-Fi connection, I'd remember all those eyes watching, all those people who'd heard me say I would do this impossible thing.

I couldn't disappoint them. More importantly, I couldn't disappoint the version of myself who'd been brave (or foolish) enough to make that promise in the first place.

The comeback journey had setbacks, tears, moments where I questioned both my sanity and my decision-making abilities. But that public declaration created momentum that carried me forward when willpower alone would have failed.

I'd love to claim I calculated all this brilliantly, that I recognized the power of public commitment and strategically wielded it like some psychological mastermind. The truth is messier and more human. Sometimes the most powerful commitments slip out when we least expect them, revealing what we truly want before our cautious minds can intervene.

So that's how I found myself on the Olympic path again, through words spoken impulsively in front of thousands, creating a commitment too public to escape. And looking back, despite how it ended (spoiler: I didn't compete in those Olympics), I wouldn't have had it any other way.

You know that moment. Words leave your mouth and suddenly gain weight, like they've been dipped in concrete. The casual "I'll run a marathon this year" that slips out at Thanksgiving dinner. The bold "I'm writing a novel" that you announce at your high school reunion, probably fueled by two glasses of wine.

Something shifts the instant those words hit air. Your private thought—once safely cocooned in the boundless realm of good intentions and someday-maybes—suddenly exists in the wild. It has witnesses now. It has expectations hanging off it like price tags. Your weightless daydream just sprouted gravity.

This is the strange magic of public commitment. Your brain immediately registers that other people now expect something of you, and the internal accounting changes completely. The cost of quitting skyrockets. It's no longer just you who would know about the dusty treadmill or the guitar gathering cobwebs in the corner. Now there's an audience—whether it's one trusted friend or an arena full of teenagers—keeping a mental scorecard.

But since this tool can be so powerful, it's not something to wield carelessly. Public commitment can drive follow-through, but it can also backfire if it's used too early or too often. Not every passing interest deserves a declaration. Going public with a goal before you've decided you actually want it can trap you in a performance loop, trying to keep up appearances rather than pursuing what genuinely matters. That's why it's worth pausing to ask: **Am I truly committed to this—or just curious, intrigued, maybe even flattered by the idea of being someone who does this thing?**

Think about the last time you told someone about a goal that actually mattered to you. Feel how the air changed afterward? The goal stayed exactly the same, but you transformed. Maybe you felt that familiar flutter of panic, the same one that hit Shawn as she hobbled offstage. Maybe you felt a surge of determination so strong it surprised you. Either way, something fundamental shifted in your relationship to that commitment the moment it escaped your thoughts and became public property.

The reasons are deliciously human: We desperately want to appear consistent and to avoid cognitive dissonance. We'd rather eat glass than face the judgment that comes with visible failure. We'll do almost anything to avoid that awkward conversation where someone cheerfully asks, "Hey, whatever happened with that business you were starting?"

But something deeper operates here too. When we speak our commitments aloud, we're forcing ourselves to get specific. The vague notion of "eating better" suddenly requires definition when you tell your lunch group you're eliminating sugar. The fuzzy "spend more time with family" crystallizes into something concrete when you announce you're leaving work at 5 p.m. sharp every Tuesday and Thursday.

Public commitments are precision instruments. They slice through our comfortable ambiguity, demanding details and timelines. They transform the abstract into something you can actually grab on to—handholds for both you and your witnesses.

This explains why wedding vows are taken in front of crowds rather than whispered privately. Why recovery programs build sharing into their DNA. Why athletes hold press conferences to announce their goals before seasons even start. These rituals are psychological technology, refined over centuries of human experience, designed to build bridges between wanting something and actually doing it.

You've been using this tool already, probably without realizing its power. The diet that finally stuck after you told your spouse. The smoking habit you kicked after promising your kids. The degree you completed because you'd already announced your enrollment on social media and couldn't bear the thought of explaining why you quit.

The real question is how to wield this force deliberately instead of stumbling into it accidentally. How do you harness the motivating pressure without setting yourself up for public failure? How do you choose the right audience, time your announcement, and calibrate the details for the right goal?

That's what we're here to figure out. Because the difference between another abandoned resolution and genuine life change might be as simple as choosing the right moment to open your mouth and let your commitment breathe in the wild.

 I still remember the weight of that ring box in my pocket. The physical weight was laughable—the thing was tiny—but the emotional gravity threatened to pull me through the floor. I'd mapped out my proposal timeline with military precision: December, a full eight months away. The ring was stashed, my master plan locked in my head. I'd shared my intentions with exactly one person: my mentor, Uncle Jim.

Here's what I learned: Commitments grow legs the moment they leave your brain and wander into someone else's consciousness.

"Why wait until December?" Uncle Jim asked, raising his eyebrows the way older and wiser folks do when they're about to detonate your perfectly reasonable plans with an unreasonably simple question. I fumbled through some half-baked explanation about timing and logistics and waiting for the perfect moment.

"What about tomorrow?" he pressed. "Isn't Shawn throwing the first pitch at Wrigley Field?"

Just like that, my beautifully orchestrated eight-month timeline imploded into twenty-four hours. The commitment had been real in my head. It had been real when I bought the ring. But sharing it with someone else transformed it into something alive, something that demanded action.

I spent that night making frantic phone calls, half convinced a Wrigley proposal was logistically impossible, entirely convinced I'd lost my mind. By morning, I had confirmation: It could happen. The escape hatches had vanished. One conversation had bulldozed months of potential second-guessing.

This pattern has followed me through life. When I announced I was pursuing a doctorate, the commitment solidified like concrete. When we declared our podcast would drop every Wednesday without fail, it became as nonnegotiable as gravity. I've started thinking of these as strategic bridge-burning. Once I tell someone—whether one trusted friend or several thousand strangers—retreat becomes more expensive than pushing forward. Even when motivation disappears, the external architecture keeps me upright.

Football taught me this in its purest form. In college, we displayed a countdown to our biggest game—Tennessee—right there in the locker room from day one. Every player, coach, and equipment manager saw those shrinking numbers daily. That public timer created constant, gentle pressure that influenced everything: offseason workouts, practice intensity, even breakfast. That was accountability at scale—dozens of people, impossible to escape.

But sometimes one person is enough. A mentor who asks hard questions. A partner who holds you to your word. A friend who remembers. Your commitments don't need stadium announcements to grow roots. They just need to exist outside your own head.

I've learned to approach declarations strategically: Who needs to know? When should I share it? How specific should I get?

That ring in my pocket became a Wrigley Field proposal because I shared my intention with someone who could blast through my limitations. "Someday" transformed into "tomorrow" because I let the commitment breathe outside my own head.

Going public with a commitment is an art form—one that, when practiced thoughtfully, can transform vague dreams into inevitable realities. The real question is how to do it in ways that launch you forward instead of pinning you down with premature pressure.

Start by taking your commitment's temperature. Is it a tender seedling, still figuring out which way is up? Or has it grown into a sturdy sapling that can handle some wind? Baby commitments often thrive with selective sharing—a trusted mentor, a supportive partner, someone who knows how to champion without overwhelming. Remember how Andrew shared his engagement plans only with Uncle Jim before he was ready for the Wrigley Field spotlight.

Some commitments are too fragile for early scrutiny—new creative projects, budding business ideas, tentative life pivots. For these, choose confidants who know the difference between accountability and interrogation. The right people offer curiosity, not critique. They ask about your novel's progress without demanding to read chapter one.

But what about those commitments that have outgrown their private cocoons? The half-marathon you've been secretly training for. The career change you've been researching during late-night rabbit holes. The lifestyle shift you've been quietly testing for months. These battle-tested commitments often flourish with broader declarations; they're one way to ask for help in the form of accountability. You tell people, "Here's where I am, here's where I want to be," and then you have that conversation.

Here's your strategic playbook for going public:

CHOOSE YOUR AUDIENCE CAREFULLY

Different communities offer different superpowers. Your family brings emotional support through the inevitable rough patches. Your professional network provides practical resources and connections. Online communities deliver daily check-ins and specialized expertise. All these audiences can add either wanted or unwanted feedback. Match the audience to whatever type of accountability your particular commitment craves.

GET SPECIFIC OR GO HOME

Vague intentions spawn vague responsibilities. "I'm working on my health" invites neither celebration nor concern when progress stalls. But "I'm eliminating processed sugar for ninety days starting Monday" creates crystal-clear parameters for both you and your witnesses.

MAKE YOUR PROGRESS IMPOSSIBLE TO IGNORE

Andrew's Tennessee countdown worked because it was unavoidable—numbers shrinking daily where everyone could see them. Replicate this through public tracking: a fundraising thermometer for your charity run, weekly social media updates about your writing streak, a shared calendar displaying your meditation consistency. These visible markers transform private habits into public performances.

SHARE THE WHY, NOT JUST THE WHAT

When you declare your commitment, include the deeper story—how it connects to your values, who it might help, what it could unlock. This creates resilience when motivation goes on vacation. Your audience won't just be tracking completion; they'll be invested in your bigger purpose.

MASTER THE ART OF STAGED DECLARATIONS

Before announcing "I'm starting a business,"

try "I'm researching market gaps this month." Before declaring "I'm writing a book," share "I'm outlining by Friday." These incremental public commitments build momentum without the paralysis that sometimes comes with premature grand announcements.

LEVERAGE YOUR BRAIN'S OBSESSION WITH CONSISTENCY

Once you've publicly declared yourself a runner, a writer, an entrepreneur, a more present parent—your brain scrambles to maintain that identity. Frame commitments in terms of who you're becoming, rather than just what you're doing. "I'm someone who prioritizes health" lands differently than "I'm trying to eat better."

And if you find yourself in Shawn's shoes—having blurted out a commitment that surprised even you—honor the wisdom in that spontaneous declaration. Trust the part of you that was brave enough to speak before your cautious mind could intervene.

PUBLIC COMMITMENTS GAIN WEIGHT. Sharing intentions dramatically increases follow-through compared to keeping them safely locked in your head where they can't judge you.

GET SPECIFIC OR GO HOME. "I'm eliminating processed sugar for ninety days starting Monday" creates clear accountability. "I'll exercise more" creates enough escape routes for a prison break.

TIME YOUR SHARING STRATEGICALLY. Baby commitments need selective sharing with trusted supporters. Battle-tested commitments benefit from broader declarations.

CHOOSE YOUR AUDIENCE CAREFULLY. Family provides emotional support through rough patches. Professional networks offer resources and connections. Online communities deliver daily check-ins and specialized expertise.

SHARE THE WHY, NOT JUST THE WHAT. Including your deeper purpose creates resilience when motivation takes a vacation. Your audience becomes invested in your bigger story.

FRAME IT AS IDENTITY. "I'm someone who prioritizes health" leverages your brain's obsession with consistency better than "I'm trying to eat better" ever could.

BEWARE PREMATURE SHARING. Half-formed ideas shared too early may wither under scrutiny before they've developed roots strong enough to handle exposure.

13

Environment

 The first time it happened, I was fifteen. The American Cup—my debut in senior competition—stretched before me like Everest viewed from base camp. This wasn't just another gymnastics meet; it was my audition for the Olympic-level arena, my first impression on the selection committee who held my future in their clipboards.

Training camp had been going like a dream. My routines were crisp; my confidence was soaring. Then, two days before competition, something inexplicable happened on the uneven bars.

There's this release move I'd nailed thousands of times—let go of the bar, execute a half-turn midair, catch the bar again. Simple as breathing. Routine as brushing my teeth. Until suddenly, terrifyingly, it wasn't.

As I prepared to release, my brain short-circuited.

My body forgot which way was up, which hand was dominant. Imagine tying your shoes every morning for fifteen years, then one day staring at the laces like they're written in ancient Sanskrit. Sounds absurd, right? Welcome to my new reality.

I fell. Hard.

My coach stared at me like I'd just announced I was quitting gymnastics to become a professional mime. "What was that?" he asked.

"No big deal." I shrugged, but the seed of doubt had already burrowed deep and started growing.

The next attempt was catastrophic. My muscles seized before release, my brain firing contradictory commands like a short-circuiting robot. I'd been invaded by what gymnasts whisper about in hushed tones: "the yips," that devastating disconnect between mind and body that can obliterate careers faster than a bad landing.

Day after day, it persisted. The selection committee noticed. Whispers rippled through the training center: "If she can't fix this, we'll have to replace her." The American Cup was dissolving in my hands before I'd even stepped onto the competition floor. Somehow, through sheer determination and probably divine intervention, I managed to compete and place well enough to stay on the team—but the experience left me forever aware of how fragile confidence can be.

Yips can spread briskly through locker rooms and training facilities. You can catch them from watching a teammate struggle, from breathing in the collective anxiety that hangs in the air like fog. The brain is wickedly susceptible to suggestion, for better or worse.

Fast-forward to my comeback years later. Eighteen, chasing the Olympic dream again after injury had derailed me. The training center buzzed with elite gymnasts, all of us pushing our bodies beyond what reasonable people would consider sane. Among us was a younger gymnast—talented but drowning in severe yips on bars. Day after day, I watched her mental warfare, saw the terror in her eyes before every approach.

I felt for her—genuinely, deeply. But I also recognized something dangerous happening to me. Her doubt was seeping into my bloodstream like poison. With Olympic Trials looming, I couldn't afford mental contamination.

So I did something that still makes me cringe a little: I asked my coach for separate training times. I requested to be surgically removed from her environment—or for her to be removed from mine.

My coach understood immediately. We rearranged my schedule, and I began training alone in the predawn hours. The stillness of the gym at daybreak became my sanctuary. Without another gymnast's struggle playing on repeat in my peripheral vision, my mind cleared. My body remembered its training.

I was still around my teammates for warm-ups, still in the locker room, still offering encouragement and celebrating small wins. But during the moments when focus mattered most, I protected my own headspace.

That experience taught me something crucial: The environment around you shapes your ability to stay committed as powerfully as willpower, maybe more so. The spaces we inhabit, the routines we follow, the people we surround ourselves with are costars in our commitment stories, either amplifying our dedication or quietly sabotaging it.

Environmental design is about engineering conditions where commitment can flourish, where the path of least resistance flows toward your goals.

What's true in a gym is true in a living room. Researchers have found that cluttered, disorganized spaces make people less likely to persist on difficult tasks. Visual chaos alone drains mental resources—the same finite energy we need for maintaining commitments.

Every pile of clutter is a small tax on your attention. Every surface covered in "I'll deal with this later" is quietly competing with the things you say matter most. Clear the space, and you clear the mind. Clear the mind, and commitment has room to breathe.

That's the goal of environmental design: make the right choice the easy choice. Instead of relying on willpower—which runs out—you arrange your surroundings so commitment becomes the default. Guardrails instead of heroics.

This works because we don't decide most of what we do: Research shows that about 43 percent of daily behaviors happen automatically, cued by our surroundings. The coffee maker on your counter prompts your morning ritual. Workout clothes laid out the night before nudge you toward the gym. The fruit bowl on the table competes with the cookies in the pantry—and proximity usually wins.

These influences operate outside our awareness. People who live within a mile of grocery stores with extensive produce sections eat significantly more fruits and vegetables, regardless of their stated nutritional intentions. Convenience shapes behavior more than conviction.

Once you recognize this power, you can harness it. The most committed people are often those who've designed their environments to work with their entirely human limitations. Small, strategic changes to your surroundings can dramatically boost your ability to follow through.

This principle shows up everywhere. Communities with the longest lifespans designed environments where healthy choices feel natural—sidewalks that invite walking, community gardens that turn cooking into social activity, strong networks that weave people together. The commitment is built into the infrastructure.

That's the goal of environmental design: Let your

surroundings do the work so your willpower doesn't have to.

I learned about the power of environmental design through a $2 spreadsheet and a $200 espresso machine.

It was 2018, and I'd become acutely aware of the financial black hole labeled "Shawn's Coffee Shop Expenditures." Being the spreadsheet enthusiast I am—a trait my wife finds endlessly charming—I'd tracked these purchases with the precision of a forensic accountant building a case. The data was damning: We were spending more on fancy coffee than some small nations allocate for their entire military budget.

When I approached Shawn with my meticulously color-coded findings, I braced for resistance. What I got instead was a conversation that completely reframed the problem. Her morning coffee ritual was about connection—to the day ahead, to herself, and ideally, to me. But somehow, my wife was leaving our home every morning to find that connection elsewhere.

So we made what felt like a radical decision: We'd invest in a high-end espresso machine for our home. This wasn't just a purchase; it was environmental surgery. We were importing the coffee shop experience into our kitchen, creating a space where that morning ritual could happen together rather than in lonely isolation.

The espresso machine transformed everything. Suddenly, our mornings had a magnetic focal point. We'd stand shoulder to shoulder, grinding beans, tamping grounds, and watching liquid gold stream into warmed cups. These moments became sacred—a daily commitment to connection engineered right into our home environment.

The financial savings were substantial, sure. But the real return on investment came in ways no spreadsheet could quantify. Our machine eliminated the friction from our commitment to start each day together. Without it, we'd need heroic amounts of willpower to create this daily ritual. With it, connection became the path of least resistance.

Our commitment to this morning ritual runs so deep that we've become those slightly ridiculous people who travel with their espresso machine. Yes, we've dragged it to lake houses and family gatherings, earning eye rolls from everyone until they taste the results and suddenly become converts.

The fascinating part: By changing just one element of our physical environment, we triggered a cascade of positive changes. Our morning espresso ritual became the foundation for deeper communication. Those early conversations over coffee often set the emotional temperature for the entire day.

This is the quiet genius of environmental design. Had we simply pledged to "spend more quality time together in the mornings," we might have succeeded for a week or two before life's currents swept us back to old patterns. Instead, we changed our environment in a way that made our commitment nearly effortless to maintain. And when commitment feels effortless, it becomes something deeper: It becomes simply who you are.

Time for an honest assessment: Is your environment designed to support the commitments you claim are important to you, or is it quietly undermining them at every turn? Let's find out with a Commitment Environmental Audit—because sometimes the space between keeping and breaking promises is literally the space around you.

MAP YOUR TIME-SPACE REALITY

For three days, track where you spend your time and what activities naturally occur in those locations. You might discover you spend forty-seven minutes each day standing in your kitchen scrolling through social media, or that your "quick email check" inevitably stretches to an hour when you sit in that particular corner of the couch. These patterns may be choreographed by your environment.

IDENTIFY YOUR COMMITMENT FRICTION POINTS

For each commitment you're struggling to maintain, identify where the physical friction occurs. Is your guitar tucked away in a case in the closet, requiring six distinct actions before you can actually play it? Does preparing healthy meals involve navigating an obstacle course of kitchen implements while the takeout menus enjoy prime real estate on your refrigerator door?

The number of steps between intention and action is a surprisingly accurate predictor of whether that action will occur. Each additional step is an opportunity for your commitment to quietly slip away.

CONDUCT A VISUAL INVENTORY

Walk through your home or workspace and photograph each room. Then review these images as if you're seeing them for the first time. What messages are these spaces sending about what matters?

If someone with no prior knowledge of you examined these spaces, what commitments would they assume you value? Is your meditation cushion prominently displayed, or is your television the undisputed centerpiece of your living room? Does your desk showcase your creative projects, or is it buried under bills and junk mail?

Our environments don't just reflect our priorities—they actively shape them. The objects you see most frequently will inevitably influence what occupies your mind.

PERFORM THE COMMITMENT PATHWAY ANALYSIS

For each major commitment in your life, physically walk through the actual pathway required to engage in it. Want to exercise more? Literally walk the route from your bed to your running shoes to the door. Count the steps. Note the obstacles. Identify the decision points where you might veer off course.

Is your gym bag packed and visible, or do you need to hunt for clean workout clothes? Is your route to health a straight line or a labyrinth of potential distractions?

EXAMINE YOUR ENVIRONMENTAL TRIGGERS

Our environments are filled with cues that trigger automatic behaviors. Some are obvious (the ping of a notification), while others operate beneath awareness (the subtle anxiety induced by a cluttered space).

For one week, note what environmental cues precede both commitment-supporting and commitment-undermining behaviors. Does passing the kitchen cabinet at 3 p.m. inevitably lead to snacking? Does seeing your journal on your nightstand prompt reflection, or does the nearby TV remote usually win the attention battle?

These triggers aren't good or bad inherently—they're either aligned with your commitments or working against them.

CALCULATE YOUR COMMITMENT VISIBILITY SCORE

Assign a visibility score (1–10) to the tools, spaces, and objects associated with each of your core commitments. The things we see regularly have a disproportionate influence on our behavior.

What you see most often is what you'll think about most often. If your laptop is more visible than your family photos, your attention will follow.

After completing this audit, you'll likely discover that your environment contains both commitment allies and commitment adversaries. The difference between someone who maintains commitments and someone who doesn't is often whether their environment makes their commitments the path of least resistance.

It might sound simplistic—that something like a photo frame or where your phone charges could influence your deepest commitments. But the research is clear, and so is our experience: environments nudge. Tiny cues accumulate into habits, patterns, priorities. It's worth paying attention.

Three years. That's how long it took me to fully shake the yips after they first ambushed me in Kansas City.

Three years of my brain inexplicably forgetting how to perform a motion I'd executed flawlessly thousands of times since high school. Three years of wondering if my body would betray me at the worst possible moment. Three years of watching the confidence I'd built over a lifetime leak away like air from a punctured tire.

The most maddening part? I could snap a football perfectly in practice. I could do it warming up. I could do it in my sleep. But when the stadium filled and the pressure mounted, something in my brain would whisper: "Hey, what if we tried something completely different this time? What if we wore gloves? What if we changed our stance? What if we reinvented the wheel at the exact moment the wheel needs to, you know, actually roll?"

And yet, somehow I found my way back. Through changing my environment.

When I landed in Washington after being cut nine times (I'm definitely counting), I encountered a kicker whose approach to pressure was fundamentally different from anything I'd seen before. Here was a guy who treated walking onto the field like strolling into his living room—comfortable, confident, at ease. He'd be playing ping-pong minutes before game time, chatting and laughing on the sidelines until the moment his number was called.

I once asked him if he ever got nervous.

"Oh yeah, dude," he said. "I get super nervous."

This surprised me. His demeanor suggested otherwise.

"But that means I'm in the zone," he continued, unfazed. "That means my body's ready. I just need to let the thousands of reps do their work. Let me take my head out of it."

While the kicker I'd previously worked with would sprint onto the field and sprint off as quickly as possible—treating the whole experience like a trip to the dentist—this guy would saunter out, dap people up, and act like he'd been there before. Because he had. And so had I.

That environment changed everything for me. His confidence was a practice, a perspective he'd cultivated—and in his presence, I began to cultivate it too. His approach to pressure became contagious in the best way, the polar opposite of how the yips had spread in Shawn's training group.

We all have yips—something that should be easy but suddenly isn't. You know the feeling. Maybe it's how you freeze before a hard conversation. Or how you pass your spouse in the hallway when things are tense, and neither of you says a word.

Whatever your personal yips might be, there's tremendous power in surrounding yourself with people who have mastered what you're struggling with. Their mastery illuminates the path. Their confidence shows you what's possible. The right people in your environment transform the impossible into the inevitable. And while you're asking whether you're surrounded by the right people, it's worth asking: Are you becoming that kind of person for someone else? Because in a healthy environment, confidence is contagious.

So as you think about designing your environment to support your commitments, don't limit yourself to rearranging furniture or optimizing your calendar. Consider also the human elements of your environment. Who makes you better simply by being around them? Who shows you what's possible? Whose approach to life makes you think, "I want some of whatever they're having"? Sometimes the most powerful environmental change is finding your way to people who help you find your way back to yourself.

None of us develops in isolation. We are, each of us, both influenced by and influencing the environments we inhabit. So choose wisely. Design thoughtfully. The spaces you build will build you.

YOUR SPACE IS EITHER HELPING OR SABOTAGING. The environments you inhabit shape commitment as powerfully as willpower. They're never neutral.

CLUTTER DRAINS THE SAME TANK. Visual chaos reduces people's ability to persist on difficult tasks by 34 percent. Disorganized spaces consume the mental energy needed for maintaining commitments.

DESIGN FOR LEAST RESISTANCE. Make your desired behaviors the easiest choice. Set out workout clothes the night before. Move the TV to a less central location. Become an architect of your own defaults.

CUES HIJACK BEHAVIOR. Forty-three percent of daily actions are habitual responses to environmental prompts. The coffee maker beckons from your counter. The fruit bowl whispers louder than hidden cookies.

PEOPLE ARE CONTAGIOUS. The humans around you spread their confidence, doubt, habits, and approaches to pressure. Their mindsets infiltrate yours whether you realize it or not.

PROXIMITY TRUMPS WILLPOWER. Living near environments that support your goals dramatically increases follow-through, regardless of stated intentions. Sometimes protection requires separation.

14

—

Mentors

There's a particular look that crosses someone's face when they're about to tell you something you don't want to hear. Equal parts compassion and steel, the expression of someone who cares enough about you to risk making you temporarily hate them. We've both seen that look countless times, usually milliseconds before a mentor delivered exactly the kind of truth we needed.

The word "mentor" has gotten a makeover in recent years. In our LinkedIn-obsessed world, it's been sanitized into coffee chats and networking—someone who opens doors and offers gentle encouragement. The mentors who've actually shaped our lives are different. They're more like spiritual chiropractors, willing to apply whatever pressure is needed to snap you back into alignment. The cracking sound is part of the process.

What does that pressure actually look like? It's

someone holding up a mirror to show you what you're actually doing versus what you think you're doing. It's uncomfortable truths delivered at precisely the moment you need them, and not a moment later.

The mentors who transformed us shared a few unmistakable traits. They possessed what we call "productive impatience"—a loving refusal to let us settle for our current level of effort. They operated from unshakable conviction about what was possible, often seeing capabilities we couldn't detect ourselves. And they were willing to risk our temporary displeasure for our long-term growth. That's a rare combination: someone who sees more in you than you see in yourself, and who cares enough to push.

Engaging with this kind of mentor is itself an act of commitment. You're giving them permission to call you forward into the version of yourself you're still becoming. That takes trust. It takes humility. And it takes choosing wisely.

So choose someone you'd like to become similar to. Engage with them. Trust them. And realize: In many ways, they are also choosing you.

I thought I knew what hard work looked like when I rolled into Vanderbilt as a cocky freshman. I'd survived what felt like a gladiatorial high school football program, and while I expected college to be tougher—better athletes, more sophisticated training, classes that actually required studying—I figured it would be a manageable step up from what I'd already conquered. I was mentally prepared for "hard," just maybe one level past my comfort zone.

Then James Franklin showed up and completely obliterated my understanding of everything.

My first clue that we'd entered an alternate dimension came during our inaugural workout under his regime. It was scheduled for 4:30 a.m. in the basketball gym, which already felt like cruel and unusual punishment. But walking into that space, I noticed something that should have sent me running: five or six trash cans positioned strategically around the gym like little monuments to human suffering. I didn't think much of it at first. By the end of that session, every single trash can had multiple heads hanging over it, mine definitely included.

Franklin had taken what our previous coach considered an intense workout and made it look like a warm-up. This was about breaking us down to our molecular components and rebuilding us according to his blueprint.

But the physical torture was just the warm-up act. Franklin implemented what he called "training rules," and they were comprehensive enough to make a monastery seem relaxed. No alcohol. Curfews that would make your mom proud. And here's the part that really captured our attention:

He sent coaches out to patrol the town and make sure we weren't partying. For college football players accustomed to a certain amount of freedom, this felt like we'd accidentally enrolled in a military academy.

Nobody liked him those first few months. By the end of our first team meeting, the consensus was crystal clear: This was absolutely not going to be fun.

Of course, some guys tested the boundaries. That's what college kids do: They probe to see if rules are actually rules or just strongly worded suggestions. Franklin's response was swift and merciless. Five a.m. workouts for a week. Additional conditioning that made regular practice feel like a spa day. Public accountability that made you wish you'd just stayed in bed forever. He wasn't bluffing about anything, and it didn't take long for everyone to get that memo.

For about six months, I can honestly say it was pure misery. Everything felt harder than necessary, more regimented than reasonable, more demanding than seemed remotely fair. But somewhere in that sustained discomfort, something unexpected started happening. We began to trust the process, even when we couldn't understand it.

Franklin had a supernatural ability to communicate absolute conviction in his vision. He acted like our success was inevitable—as long as we followed his system. That confidence was infectious, even when the system itself felt designed by someone who clearly hated sleep and joy.

Meanwhile, I was quietly imploding in the classroom. I was failing three of my four classes that first semester—organic chemistry, multivariable calculus, physics. The one class I wasn't failing was the easy one, which somehow made everything worse. I was seriously tempted to transfer to somewhere with lower academic standards and more reasonable workout times. My academic approach wasn't working, football felt like daily punishment, and I wasn't having any fun. It felt like a complete life disaster.

Instead of offering sympathy or suggesting I lower my expectations, Franklin gave me something more valuable: a system. He set up tutors. He provided actual templates for how to communicate with professors when traveling for games. Most importantly, he sat me down and said, "Here's exactly what you should do," with the tone of someone sharing battle-tested strategies.

"Go talk to your professor," he'd say. "Propose some solutions. Walk through what you're struggling with. Come up with a list." It wasn't revolutionary advice, but it was the first time anyone had given me a concrete framework for approaching academic challenges instead of just hoping things would magically work out.

The transformation took weeks of grinding through Franklin's academic road map, questioning whether any of it would actually work or if I was just delaying the inevitable academic apocalypse. I'd drag myself to tutoring sessions, visit professors during office hours, implement his communication strategies even when they felt awkward and overly formal. Sometimes I wanted to skip the extra work or avoid the difficult conversations entirely.

Franklin created an environment where commitment became contagious. When you're surrounded by teammates grinding through 5 a.m. workouts and mandatory study halls, when your coach checks your progress with the same intensity he brings to reviewing game film, quitting starts to feel like swimming upstream against a very strong current.

The breakthrough came gradually, then all at once. Calculus concepts fell into place like puzzle pieces. Chemistry grades improved from disastrous to merely concerning to actually respectable. Professors responded positively to my outreach efforts. By year's end, I was actually engaged with material that had once felt impossibly abstract.

I went from failing three classes to graduating early, getting into Vanderbilt's business school, and earning conference academic player honors. The real victory was discovering my capacity for sustained commitment when the right structures existed to support it.

Franklin's gift was seeing a version of me that didn't exist yet, then systematically removing every excuse I had for not becoming that person. When he looked at a failing freshman, he didn't see a lost cause. He saw someone who hadn't learned how to commit yet. That "yet" made all the difference.

For me, that mentor was Coach Liang Chow. I was five years old when I first walked into his gym, and twenty when I walked out for the last time. Fifteen years—nearly my entire childhood and adolescence—shaped by a man who understood that true commitment isn't about forcing yourself through misery, but about creating conditions where dedication feels as natural as breathing.

Chow's genius lay in how he engineered commitment itself. His rules were deceptively simple: show respect and be on time. But beneath this simplicity was a sophisticated understanding of how sustained dedication actually works. He knew that commitment thrives when expectations are crystal clear, consequences are absolute, and trust runs deep.

The gym's most powerful rule illustrated this perfectly: If you ever walked out of practice—just left, without a word—you never came back.

Ever.

This sounds cruel, but in reality, it created clarity. The rule eliminated the mental escape hatch that undermines so many commitments. When leaving isn't really an option, staying becomes your only choice, and you learn to work through problems instead of fleeing from them.

I watched this play out with other gymnasts over the years. Someone would get overwhelmed, storm out in a moment of emotion, and that would be it. No negotiations, no second chances, no dramatic comeback stories. What these departures taught the rest of us was profound: Commitment means staying present when things get difficult—especially when they get difficult. It's a lesson that served me far beyond gymnastics: in marriage, in business, in every area where quitting feels temporarily easier than continuing.

Because we knew the only real choice was to stay and work through challenges, we stopped wasting mental energy on escape routes and focused entirely on how to improve. The irrevocable nature of our commitment became its own kind of freedom.

The time boundaries helped too. Practice ran from 4 to 8 p.m., precisely. No exceptions, no extensions, no starting early. This predictability let us commit completely within those hours, knowing exactly what was expected and for how long. When commitment has clear parameters, you can give everything you have.

But Chow's most revolutionary insight was about what we should be committing to in the first place. While other elite coaches measured success through scores and rankings, Chow cared exclusively about effort and attention to the fundamentals. He would tell us repeatedly that our scores were meaningless to him—only how hard we tried mattered. This was a fundamental reframing of what deserved our dedication.

This distinction changed everything about how commitment felt day-to-day. When your effort gets evaluated rather than your results, you can throw yourself completely into the work without the anxiety that comes from obsessing over outcomes you can't fully control. We learned to commit to the process, which paradoxically made both the process more enjoyable and the outcomes more achievable.

Chow enforced this value system through his consequences. I learned this viscerally the day I cheated on conditioning repetitions. His response was immediate: a fifteen-minute handstand. For reference, I could do a two-minute handstand without thinking, a five-minute handstand with ease, and a ten-minute handstand with effort. So, while doable, a fifteen-minute handstand was hard and consumed a lot of precious practice time. And if I dropped before time was up, I would leave permanently.

It was harsh by today's standards, but it taught me something crucial about the relationship between integrity and commitment. Real commitment requires honesty about your effort, especially when no one is watching.

The beauty of Chow's approach was how it created space for genuine joy within serious dedication. He would tell us to get our work done efficiently so we could "go to Dairy Queen"— and he meant it literally. After a focused practice, he'd pile us into his car and drive to Dairy Queen. Sometimes he'd cut training short as a reward. The message was clear: Commit fully, and there's room for joy.

This taught us that commitment and pleasure are partners. When you commit fully during work time, play time becomes truly restorative. And part of what made those Dairy Queen trips so sweet was how rare they were. A treat, after all, isn't a treat if you have it every day. We learned to work with adult-level intensity so we could play with childlike freedom. The commitment enhanced the joy instead of diminishing it.

Perhaps most importantly, Chow taught us that athletic commitment should serve our larger life commitments. He was the first person to tell me I would attend an Ivy League college, years before I understood what that meant. Education came before gymnastics, always. If grades slipped, we left practice immediately until they improved.

This hierarchy of commitments created a framework that lasted far beyond my competitive career. Chow was teaching us to commit strategically—to understand which commitments serve our deepest values and which ones might distract from them.

I didn't fully understand what Chow had given me until I stood on the Olympic floor. The lights, the crowd, the pressure—and somehow, I felt like a kid again, just playing. That was his gift. He'd taught me that when you commit completely in practice, performance becomes freedom. You're not trying to prove anything. You've already done the work.

I still hear his voice. I probably always will.

Both Franklin and Chow operated within institutional frameworks—football programs and gymnastics academies with built-in structures for mentorship. Their authority was clear; their roles were defined; their ability to set standards was largely unquestioned. But some of the most transformative mentoring happens outside these formal relationships, when someone chooses to invest in your growth without any official obligation to do so.

We discovered this during a seemingly casual conversation in the back of an SUV, driving through the mountains of Utah with a venture capitalist we'd just met on a television show. Jeremy Bloom had been an NFL player and Olympic skier, so we shared the common language of elite athletics, as well as entrepreneurship.

The conversation started innocuously. We shared what we thought were ambitious plans for our media company. Jeremy listened, then asked the kind of specific questions that make you squirm. How much did we want to make annually? What kind of company valuation were we targeting? Who were the five most successful people in our immediate circle, and what were their businesses worth?

We answered as honestly as we could, proud of our carefully considered goals. Jeremy's response was swift and unforgiving: "That's way too small." With just four words, he fundamentally rejected our entire framework of success.

Jeremy had no formal authority over us, no ability to create consequences for ignoring his advice. His power came entirely from our recognition that he'd achieved things we wanted to achieve, and his willingness to tell us truths that no one else would voice.

The discomfort was immediate. We'd spent months on these goals, proud of how big we were dreaming. To have someone we respected wave them away felt like whiplash. But Jeremy wasn't finished. He started describing what successful entrepreneurs actually built, and suddenly our big dreams looked like rounding errors.

What made this mentorship so powerful was its timing. We were at a crossroads professionally, successful enough to be confident but still moldable enough to pivot. Jeremy caught us at the exact moment when we were ready to hear that our current trajectory, while good, could be extraordinary with the right adjustments.

Unlike our athletic mentors, Jeremy couldn't create practice schedules or training regimens to support our new commitments. Instead, he offered something more subtle and perhaps more valuable: He expanded our conception of what deserved our dedication. He helped us see that committing to small goals was just as much work as committing to transformational ones, and significantly less rewarding.

This insight shifted everything about how we approached our business. We stopped thinking incrementally and started thinking exponentially. We began asking different questions, seeking different advisers, making different trade-offs with our time and attention. The commitment to growth intensified, but the target of that commitment had fundamentally changed.

Our conversation with Jeremy lasted maybe thirty minutes, but it redirected years of our professional lives. We learned that informal mentorship can be just as transformative as formal coaching, that the right question at the right moment can be worth more than months of regular guidance.

Perhaps most importantly, Jeremy showed us that great mentors help you discover goals worthy of your deepest commitment. They see potential you've overlooked and challenge you to reorganize your life around possibilities you hadn't considered.

This is what exceptional mentors ultimately provide: a vision of your actual capacity, and the loving insistence that you build a life to match it.

Looking back across these relationships—Franklin with his 4:30 a.m. workouts and systematic approach to excellence, Chow with his fifteen-year commitment to character over performance, Jeremy with his casual demolition of our too-small dreams—we see a pattern rooted in their shared audacity.

They saw us clearly—flaws, inconsistencies, rough edges, and all—and believed anyway. Their optimism was radical and discerning, anchored in a deep understanding of our potential. They held an unwavering conviction that we were capable of sustained commitment to something extraordinary, even when we had no evidence to support it ourselves.

They understood something about human nature that we're still learning. Most people struggle with commitment because they've committed themselves to goals that are either too small to sustain their interest or too vague to guide their daily choices. The right mentor helps you find commitments worth having.

This may explain why real mentors are becoming rarer. With endless advice and infinite content available online, the mentor's role seems almost obsolete. Why do you need someone to guide your commitments when you can Google best practices, watch YouTube tutorials, or join online communities for any pursuit imaginable?

Information alone doesn't create transformation.

Knowledge alone doesn't build commitment. And no algorithm can look you in the eye and tell you that your current trajectory, while comfortable, falls short of your actual potential.

The mentors who shaped us transferred conviction. They modeled what it looked like to care deeply about something, to organize your entire life around principles that mattered, to show up consistently when motivation flagged.

In the end, the greatest gift these mentors gave us was their refusal to accept our excuses for living smaller lives than we were capable of living. They saw us more clearly than we saw ourselves, and they wouldn't let us forget what they saw.

REAL MENTORS ARE SPIRITUAL CHIROPRACTORS. They see where you're out of alignment and apply the pressure needed to snap you back into place, even when it hurts.

THEY BELIEVE IN A VERSION OF YOU THAT DOESN'T EXIST YET. Great mentors see potential you couldn't detect with a microscope. They set standards you haven't even imagined are possible.

PRODUCTIVE IMPATIENCE DRIVES TRANSFORMATION. Exceptional mentors refuse to let you settle for your current level of effort. They create urgency around your own potential.

THEY ENGINEER INEVITABILITY. Through crystal-clear expectations and systematic removal of escape routes, they make quitting harder than continuing. When leaving truly isn't an option, you stop wasting energy on whether to quit and focus on how to improve.

THEY EXPAND YOUR SENSE OF SCALE. Committing to small goals takes the same energy as committing to transformational ones. The right mentor asks: Why dream small?

OPENNESS MATTERS MORE THAN AGE. The most transformative relationships begin when you're genuinely moldable, willing to have assumptions challenged and patterns reshaped.

Metrics

The alarm clock buzzes, and I can hear my dad already moving around downstairs. By the time I stumble into the kitchen, rubbing sleep from my eyes, he's already got the tandem bike rolled out to the driveway, checking tire pressure with the methodical precision of a pit crew chief.

"Ready to beat yesterday's time?" he calls out, that familiar glint of competition in his voice.

This was our morning ritual throughout elementary school—Dad and me on a bright gray tandem bicycle, racing against the clock on our way to school. He would rotate among my siblings throughout the week, but when it was my turn, the whole nineteen-minute journey became this delicious tension between getting to school and proving we could shave off a few seconds from our previous best.

"JD and I did it in seventeen minutes yesterday," he'd announce as we clipped into the pedals. "Let's see if we can beat it."

Dad would call out our splits at every familiar landmark, his voice carrying that mix of encouragement and genuine excitement that made even a Tuesday morning feel like the Olympics. The stopwatch in his hand turned our ordinary commute into an extraordinary adventure.

Looking back, I realize my father was teaching me about the relationship between measurement and commitment. He carried that same approach into everything—timing his daily walks with my mom, tracking how many nights we spent at the lake house versus at home, even maintaining what would become a 473-day streak of writing daily devotionals to people in his construction business (a story we'll explore more later).

This is the power of metrics in the service of commitment. When we measure the things that matter to us, we create a feedback loop that makes our abstract intentions tangible and our long-term goals achievable through daily actions.

That's because metrics provide something our emotions and intuitions cannot—objective feedback about whether our efforts actually work. They cut through the fog of busyness and self-deception to reveal the truth about our progress.

The magic happens when measurement meets commitment. Suddenly, abstract goals become concrete actions. Vague aspirations transform into specific behaviors you can track, adjust, and improve. That morning workout becomes data point number 47 in a larger story of showing up for yourself.

But here's what my dad understood about tracking those morning bike rides: The best metrics feel like games. They turn the ordinary work of commitment into something engaging, even exciting. When you're racing against yesterday's version of yourself, improvement becomes its own reward.

This is about recognizing that the things we commit to deserve our attention—and that attention, when systematically applied, has the power to transform both our habits and ourselves.

The lessons learned from those morning bike rides extend far beyond childhood games. When measurement becomes a tool for commitment rather than mere competition, it transforms from a simple habit into a powerful mechanism for sustained change. But is there actual evidence that tracking our efforts strengthens our ability to stick with what matters most?

The answer lies in decades of behavioral psychology research that reveals that the simple act of paying attention to our progress fundamentally changes our relationship with our goals. Dr. Albert Bandura's landmark research examined what separates people who successfully maintain long-term behavioral changes from those who abandon their commitments after initial enthusiasm fades.

The key differentiator wasn't willpower, motivation, or even the strength of their initial desire for change. It was self-monitoring through systematic measurement. Participants who tracked their progress toward goals—whether losing weight, learning new skills, or changing ingrained habits—showed significantly higher rates of sustained commitment compared to those who relied solely on internal drive or good intentions.

The research revealed what Bandura termed a "self-regulatory feedback loop." When people measured their efforts consistently, they created an ongoing dialogue between their actions and their aspirations. This awareness of progress strengthened their resolve during difficult moments. And when the numbers disappointed, something surprising happened: The discrepancy fueled determination. A lower-than-expected result became a signal. The very act of measuring made people more inclined to adjust, adapt, and act. The gap between where they were and where they wanted to be became a source of energy.

But the studies uncovered something even more intriguing: The type of measurement mattered enormously. Participants who tracked process metrics—actions they could control daily—maintained their commitments far longer than those who focused solely on outcome metrics. The person who counted workouts completed stayed committed longer than the person who only stepped on the scale. The aspiring writer who tracked pages written each day persisted longer than the one who only monitored acceptance letters from publishers.

When people track their efforts rather than just their results, they maintain agency over their progress. They can celebrate showing up consistently even when outcomes remain uncertain. They build confidence through accumulated evidence of their own reliability, independent of external validation or immediate success.

Studies of habit formation show that people who measure small, daily actions—taking vitamins, doing push-ups, writing thank-you notes—maintain these behaviors at rates three times higher than those who simply commit to the behavior without tracking it. The measurement provides what researchers call "behavioral scaffolding," a sort of game within the game that makes abstract commitments concrete and manageable.

Perhaps most surprisingly, the research suggests that measurement works precisely because it makes our commitments visible to ourselves. Many people struggle with what psychologists call "commitment invisibility"—the tendency to lose track of whether they're actually following through on their stated priorities amid the noise and complexity of daily life. Without measurement, genuine effort can feel ineffective, and actual progress can go unnoticed.

This body of research points to a simple but powerful truth: Measurement transforms commitment from an abstract intention into a tangible practice.

The research makes perfect sense to me because I've lived it. But what took me years to understand is that while measurement works for the obvious stuff—workouts completed, books read, calories consumed—the real magic happens when you start tracking the things that actually matter most: love, connection, joy, and the thousands of small moments that build a meaningful life.

Shawn and I discovered this somewhat by accident. After retiring from sports, we felt rudderless without the clear metrics that had defined our athletic careers. How do you measure success when there's no scoreboard, no personal records to chase, no rankings to climb? We started tracking everything we could think of, initially as a way to bring some structure back into our lives.

What began as a desperate attempt to feel productive quickly evolved into something far more profound. We found ourselves measuring date nights per month, family dinners eaten together as a group of five, thank-you texts sent to friends. We tracked how many times we called our parents each week, how many homemade lunches we packed for the kids, how many bedtime stories we read aloud.

At first, friends thought we'd lost our minds. "You track how many game nights you have?" they'd ask, equal parts amused and horrified. "What's next, measuring hugs?" (For the record, we never measured hugs, though we did briefly consider it.)

But something beautiful started happening. The act of tracking these softer metrics revealed patterns we'd never noticed. In the months when we hit our target of six family dinners per week, the kids seemed happier, more talkative, more connected to what was happening in each other's lives. When we consistently managed four date nights per month, Shawn and I felt more like partners and less like ships passing in the night.

The numbers became our early-warning system. One particularly busy season, we realized we'd been hanging out with friends constantly—double dates, group dinners, weekend gatherings. It felt social and fun, but when I looked at our tracking sheet, I saw we'd had exactly zero nights of just our family of five. No wonder Shawn couldn't tell you what our daughter, Drew, had done at school that week. We were prioritizing friendships over family intimacy.

The beauty of measuring these "soft" commitments is that it forces you to define what you actually value, rather than what you think you should value. Before we started tracking, I would have sworn we prioritized family time. But the data revealed a different story. Good intentions, it turns out, don't automatically translate into consistent actions.

Take our commitment to gratitude. We'd read all the research about the benefits of expressing appreciation, and we genuinely wanted to be more grateful people. But "being grateful" is abstract. "Sending three thank-you texts per week to friends" is concrete. Suddenly, gratitude became a practice instead of just a nice idea.

The metrics also revealed unexpected connections. The weeks when we hit our target for individual time with each child correlated strongly with better family dinner conversations. When we consistently did our morning coffee and devotional time together, we argued less about logistics later in the day. The data showed us how different commitments reinforced each other in ways we'd never consciously recognized.

That's the real power of metrics applied to love and relationships: They make the invisible visible. How often do we truly connect with our spouse beyond logistics? How frequently do we create space for unstructured play with our children? How consistently do we invest in friendships that matter? Without measurement, these questions stay comfortably vague. With measurement, they become commitments we can actually keep.

My dad grasped this intuitively. Those tandem bike rides with the stopwatch? He was measuring connection, adventure, shared accomplishment—the commute to school was just the vehicle. That simple act of tracking transformed an ordinary morning routine into a tradition I'm still talking about decades later.

Here's what surprised us: Tracking these metrics makes relationships more joyful. When you're consciously trying to hit twelve game nights per year with your kids, you start looking forward to family game night differently. Each one becomes evidence of the kind of parent you're choosing to become.

What gets measured gets treasured. And the people we love deserve at least as much intentionality as we bring to everything else.

The beauty of measurement lies in its simplicity, but that same simplicity can feel overwhelming when you're staring at a blank spreadsheet, wondering where to begin. The key is starting small and specific rather than attempting to track everything at once.

Begin with a single commitment that matters to you but feels frustratingly abstract. Ask yourself: What's one area of my life where I keep saying "I should do this more" but can't quite tell if I'm actually making progress? Maybe it's being a better friend, creating more family memories, pursuing a creative passion, or simply being more present in your daily life.

Once you've identified that commitment, the next question becomes: What would consistent progress actually look like? This is where most people get stuck, trying to measure outcomes they can't fully control rather than actions they can. Instead of tracking "closer friendships" (an outcome), consider measuring "meaningful conversations initiated per week" (an action). Rather than "being a better parent" (vague), try "individual time spent with each child per month" (specific).

The most effective metrics share three characteristics: They're specific enough to count, frequent enough to provide regular feedback, and small enough that missing a day doesn't derail your entire effort. Tracking "one thank-you text per week" works better than "expressing more gratitude." Measuring "family dinners eaten together" proves more actionable than "stronger family bonds."

Start with what you can easily observe and record. If you want to commit to reading more, track pages read daily rather than books finished monthly. If you're working on your marriage, count date nights scheduled rather than relationship satisfaction scores. If you're pursuing a creative practice, measure time spent creating rather than quality of output.

The recording system matters less than consistency. A simple tally sheet on your phone works as well as an elaborate spreadsheet. Some people prefer checking boxes on a physical calendar; others use apps that send daily reminders. The best system is whichever one you'll actually use without thinking too hard about it.

Here's a practical framework to get started: Choose one commitment. Identify one specific, controllable action that supports that commitment. Pick a frequency you can realistically maintain (daily actions work well for habits, weekly counts suit relationship goals, monthly tracking serves longer-term projects). Record your metric in whatever format feels most natural.

Give yourself at least thirty days of consistent tracking before evaluating whether the metric is working. Sometimes the simple act of paying attention creates improvement before you consciously change your behavior. Other times, the measurement reveals that your chosen action doesn't actually support your deeper commitment as effectively as you'd hoped.

The goal is to create a feedback loop that helps you align your daily actions with your stated values. The measurement serves the commitment, rather than the other way around.

When my father died, he was on day 473 of writing daily devotionals to his building clients. Four hundred and seventy-three consecutive days of sitting down each morning, crafting words of encouragement and wisdom for the contractors, suppliers, and homeowners who made up his professional world.

I found the evidence of this streak scattered throughout his office—notebooks filled with handwritten drafts, emails saved in carefully organized folders, a simple calendar where he'd marked each day with a small checkmark. Day 1. Day 100. Day 250. Day 473. Each mark a small victory, a promise kept to himself and to the people who would start their day reading his words.

Dad loved telling people about his streaks. He'd announce with genuine pride that he was on day 200-something of his Duolingo practice, day 1,000-something of learning Spanish. "I'm stacking days," he'd say with that familiar glint in his eye, the same one I remembered from our tandem bike rides. The numbers mattered to him because they represented something deeper: the accumulation of small choices that, over time, created the life he wanted to live.

He applied this same methodical attention to everything that mattered. How many nights did our family spend at the lake house versus at home?

He'd track it. "This year we spent twenty-seven nights at the lake. Let's try to beat that next year." How much honey did we harvest from our beehives? He'd weigh it, record it, celebrate the abundance. How often did he and my mom take their morning walks together? Daily tallies of what mattered to him.

Those 473 devotionals were proof of his commitment to showing up, day after day, for the relationships that defined his work. Even when inspiration felt elusive, even when his building projects were stressful, even when life got complicated, he'd sit down and write. Because he'd promised himself he would. Because the streak itself had become sacred.

I think about that number often: 473. It represents more than a year and a quarter of never missing a day, never making an excuse, never deciding that just this once he could skip it. It's the physical manifestation of what we've been exploring throughout this chapter—how measurement transforms commitment from an abstract intention into a tangible practice.

But here's what moves me most about my father's legacy: He understood that the deepest commitments often require the simplest metrics. He didn't need sophisticated tracking systems or elaborate spreadsheets. He needed a calendar, a pen, and the daily choice to show up. The metric served the commitment, creating a feedback loop that sustained him through seasons when motivation alone wouldn't have been enough.

When I look at our family's own tracking practices now—our date nights, our family dinners, our individual time with each child—I see his influence everywhere. The act of counting makes the commitment concrete, turning good intentions into lived reality.

Those 473 days remind me that the most meaningful numbers aren't always the biggest ones. Sometimes they're the quiet accumulation of ordinary moments, measured one day at a time, building toward something larger than any single effort could achieve. My father stacked days until they became a legacy. What most people only aspire to, he actually lived. The stopwatch he started in my childhood is still running—now in my own family, marking time we choose to treasure.

Some streaks are worth keeping forever.

WHAT GETS MEASURED GETS TREASURED. Tracking transforms abstract commitments into concrete actions. Good intentions become lived reality.

PROCESS BEATS OUTCOME. Count workouts completed rather than obsessing over the scale. Track pages written rather than waiting for acceptance letters. Control what you can control.

THE BEST METRICS FEEL LIKE GAMES. Turn ordinary commitments into engaging challenges by racing against yesterday's version of yourself, like Andrew's morning tandem bike rides with his dad.

TRACK THE SOFT STUFF. Date nights per month. Family dinners together. Thank-you texts sent to friends. These reveal what you truly value versus what you think you should value.

START SMALL AND STAY SPECIFIC. Measure one controllable action that supports your commitment. Trying to track everything guarantees you'll track nothing.

MEASUREMENT MAKES THE INVISIBLE VISIBLE. Without tracking, genuine effort can feel ineffective and actual progress slips by unnoticed.

16

—

Belief

The night before every competition, I would walk into the gym wearing street clothes—sweatpants, sneakers, whatever I'd thrown on that morning. No leotard, no grips, no chalk. To an outsider, it probably looked like I was lost, or maybe conducting some kind of bizarre equipment inspection. But this ritual, as strange as it appeared, would become one of the most important training sessions of my gymnastics career.

My coach would call out a number—five, eight, ten, fifteen—and I knew exactly what it meant. That's how many perfect routines I needed to complete before I could leave. Mental routines.

I'd start at the vault, hoisting myself up to sit cross-legged on top of the apparatus like some kind of meditative gymnast Buddha. Then I'd close my eyes and begin the most challenging workout of my week. "Picture yourself walking into the arena tomorrow," my coach would say. "What do you hear? What do you smell? What are the judges wearing? Now, show me a perfect vault."

What happened next was a master class in mental discipline that made physical training look like a warm-up. I'd begin to visualize my approach, the springboard, the flight through the air—and inevitably, somewhere around the twist, my brain flashed a vision of me face-planting into the mat. Splat. Routine over. Start again.

"Five perfect in a row," I'd always say, even when he wasn't there. His voice was lodged somewhere in my memory, surfacing the moment my focus slipped. Five perfect reps. That was the standard. And somehow, my brain still wanted to sabotage it. But thankfully, after I'd quieted my mind and settled down, it would get easier.

The cruelty of this exercise wasn't just that I had to achieve five consecutive perfect mental routines; it was that I had to do it while sitting motionless in a gymnasium full of chaos. Other gymnasts were training around me, music was blasting, coaches were shouting corrections. And there I sat, looking like I was taking the world's most zen study break, actually engaged in what felt like mental hand-to-hand combat with my own imagination.

I'd move from vault to bars to beam to floor, sitting on each piece of equipment like it was my personal meditation cushion. By the time I reached the balance beam—four inches wide and four feet off the ground—the absurdity of my position wasn't lost on me. Here I was, a teenage girl in sweatpants, perched on gymnastics equipment, battling invisible demons that existed only in my head.

The beam was always the worst. There's something about that narrow strip of wood that invited every possible catastrophe my mind could conjure. I'd visualize my mount, stick the landing, begin my routine—and suddenly I'd be wobbling, then falling, then lying in a heap on the mat below. Reset. Try again.

At first, I thought this was ridiculous. Why was I wasting time sitting around thinking about gymnastics when I could actually be doing gymnastics? But over the months and years, something shifted. The mental reps became harder to complete than the physical ones, but they also became more powerful. I was building what my coach called "mental endurance"—the ability to push negative possibilities out of my head and replace them with positive ones.

By the time I reached the Olympics, this skill had become second nature. While other athletes were psyching themselves out in the moments before competition, I had already completed hundreds of perfect routines in my mind. I'd practiced the physical movements and the mental state required to execute them under pressure.

What my coach was teaching me—though neither of us would have called it this at the time—was belief. Not the wishful-thinking variety, but the practical kind—the ability to train your mind to rehearse success instead of failure. It's a skill that extends far beyond gymnastics, into every area where commitment is tested by uncertainty, setbacks, and the very human tendency to imagine everything that could go wrong.

This is belief as a tool, rather than a feeling. And like any tool, it can be learned, practiced, and refined.

Belief sits at the heart of every meaningful commitment. It's the thread running through a hundred quiet acts of hope: the entrepreneur sending her hundredth pitch email, the artist picking up the brush after rejection, the couple choosing each other during a hard season, the athlete lacing up for another early morning. Each one a decision to keep showing up when the outcome is uncertain.

The science here is practical. When we visualize performing an action, our brains fire many of the same neural pathways as when we actually perform it. Mental rehearsal creates real physiological changes. The gymnast sitting motionless before her routine is strengthening the neural networks she'll need, one visualization at a time.

Research from sports psychology reveals that athletes who engage in systematic mental rehearsal develop greater resilience when things go wrong. They've practiced the mental state required to persist through setbacks. Studies of successful entrepreneurs show what researchers call "optimistic persistence"—the ability to maintain belief in favorable outcomes despite mixed evidence.

Belief, in this context, means choosing which version of an uncertain future to mentally rehearse. Every commitment involves navigating unknowns, and our minds will populate those unknowns with something. The question is whether we're practicing success or disaster in the theater of our imagination.

The Marines understand this intuitively. When recruits sign their enlistment papers, they haven't yet endured boot camp or proven themselves in the field. But from day one, they call themselves Marines. That identity—assumed before it's fully earned—pulls them forward. It reshapes how they show up, how they train, how they push through pain. They claim the title, then rise to meet it.

Belief and action reinforce each other. The more we mentally rehearse success, the more likely we are to take actions that make success possible. The more we take those actions, the more evidence we accumulate that our belief was warranted. Commitment transforms from discipline into confidence.

The idea that mental rehearsal creates real physiological changes sounds compelling in theory. In practice, as I discovered during my NFL career, it's also brutally difficult—and surprisingly more demanding than any physical workout I'd ever endured.

When I was struggling with performance anxiety as a long snapper, Shawn walked me through the same mental training techniques her gymnastics coach had taught her. The concept seemed straightforward enough: Visualize successful snaps instead of letting my mind wander into disaster scenarios. How hard could it be to think about something going right?

Turns out, incredibly hard.

Picture this: I'm standing on the sideline during a timeout, knowing I'm about to walk onto the field for a game-winning field goal attempt. Eighty thousand people are screaming, the stadium lights feel like they're burning holes in my jersey, and I have about sixty seconds to get my mental house in order. This should be the perfect time to run through my visualization routine—imagine the perfect snap, the ball spiraling back to the holder exactly where it needs to be, the kick sailing through the uprights.

Instead, my brain decides this is the ideal moment to offer a comprehensive review of everything that could go wrong. What if the snap is too high? Too low? What if it's wobbly? What if I completely whiff and the ball just rolls backward? What if this becomes the moment that ends my career, replayed on ESPN for eternity as a cautionary tale about undrafted rookies who couldn't handle the pressure?

The mental reps Shawn taught me were designed to interrupt this spiral, but they required a level of cognitive discipline that made physical training look like a relaxing stroll. In the gym, if I dropped a weight or missed a rep, I could just pick it up and try again. But in my mind, if I started visualizing a perfect snap and suddenly imagined it sailing over the holder's head, I had to stop everything and start over. No shortcuts, no "close enough." It was five perfect mental reps or nothing.

The first time I tried this during an actual game situation, I made it through exactly half of one visualization before my brain helpfully inserted a montage of every bad snap I'd ever made in practice. Reset. Try again. By the time I actually walked onto the field, I'd managed maybe two clean mental reps out of the five I was aiming for, and I felt more exhausted than if I'd just run wind sprints.

But here's what I discovered: Those mental workouts were building something unexpected. Every time I caught my thoughts drifting toward catastrophe and redirected them back to the task at hand, I was strengthening a kind of mental muscle. The stamina to maintain focus when my mind wanted to run wild.

The breakthrough came during a particularly high-pressure game later that season. Walking onto the field for what would turn out to be the game-winning kick, I realized something had shifted. My mind still offered its usual menu of worst-case scenarios. But now I had a trained response. I acknowledged the doubt, then deliberately rehearsed what I wanted to happen instead.

The snap was perfect. I'd practiced choosing confidence over catastrophe so many times it had become instinctive.

The physical mechanics hadn't changed. My technique, arm strength, understanding of the fundamentals—all the same. What I'd developed was the ability to direct mental energy toward productive scenarios. And this, I realized, had applications far beyond football.

Every time I sent another business email after a string of rejections, every time I chose to see potential in a new project despite past failures, I was drawing on the same capacity. Belief is a skill. And, like any skill, it answers to practice.

In 2004, exercise physiologist Dr. Guang Yue at the Cleveland Clinic Foundation conducted a study that would challenge everything we thought we knew about the relationship between mind and muscle. His research team recruited thirty young, healthy volunteers and divided them into groups with very different training regimens. One group would spend weeks performing actual physical exercises, flexing their finger muscles and contracting their elbow muscles with maximum effort. Another group would do something that sounded almost absurd: They would sit quietly and simply imagine performing the same exercises, never moving a muscle.

Dr. Yue's team had the participants in the "mental training" group spend fifteen minutes each day for four weeks imagining themselves performing maximum voluntary contractions of their little finger abductor muscle and elbow flexor muscles. The results were remarkable: Participants who did physical exercises increased their finger abduction strength by 53 percent, while those who only imagined the exercises—never actually moving their muscles—increased their strength by 35 percent. Even more surprisingly, the mental training group showed their greatest gains four weeks after the training had ended, suggesting the brain was still building strength even after the imaginary workouts stopped.

But the truly fascinating discovery came when the researchers examined what was happening inside the participants' brains. Using advanced brain imaging, they found that when people visualized movement, the same brain regions became active as when they actually performed the physical movements. The brain showed identical activity patterns whether participants were mentally rehearsing an action or physically performing it.

What this study and others like it reveal is that belief—in the form of mental rehearsal and visualization—literally rewires the brain, creating the same neural pathways that physical practice would build. This process stimulates brain regions involved in movement rehearsal, priming the brain and body for action so that we move more effectively when the time comes to actually perform.

The research suggests that when Andrew was struggling through those mental reps on the sideline, and when Shawn was sitting motionless on gymnastics equipment visualizing perfect routines, they weren't just engaging in positive thinking. They were conducting sophisticated neural training sessions, building the same brain circuitry that physical practice would create. The mind, it turns out, is remarkably literal—it treats imagined experiences with the same neurological seriousness as real ones.

This is why belief belongs in any serious discussion of commitment tools. It's mechanical, measurable, and surprisingly practical.

The science makes clear that belief is essential for maintaining commitments. But knowing this doesn't make it easier. When your current reality feels like a string of setbacks, sitting quietly and envisioning triumph takes real effort. How do you actually build this capacity? And more practically, how do you choose what to believe in?

The process begins with clarity about your commitment itself. What specifically are you trying to achieve? The more vivid and detailed your mental picture, the more your brain has to work with. If your commitment is to write a novel, for instance, don't just imagine "being a published author." Picture yourself typing the final sentence, feeling the satisfaction of completion, holding the physical book in your hands. What does the cover look like? How does it feel to flip through pages of your own words? Where are you when you first see it in a bookstore?

Next, borrow a technique from Shawn's gymnastics training: Practice mental rehearsal sessions. Choose a quiet moment each day—perhaps first thing in the morning or right before sleep—and run through your commitment as if it's already happening. Start small: five perfect mental repetitions of success. If doubt creeps in (and it will), stop and begin again. This is about training your mind to default to possibility rather than catastrophe.

Consider the perspective you choose for these mental rehearsals. Do you see yourself from the outside, watching your success unfold like a movie? Or do you experience it from the inside, through your own eyes? Research suggests that first-person visualization—seeing through your own eyes—creates stronger neural activation. Experiment with both and notice which feels more powerful for you.

Create what you might call "evidence files"—small collections of proof that your commitment is achievable. This could be stories of others who've done what you're attempting, past successes of your own in different areas, or even small wins you've already accumulated toward this particular goal. When belief wavers, these files provide concrete reminders that what you're attempting has been done before and can be done again.

Finally, develop a ritual around moments of doubt. Instead of fighting negative thoughts, acknowledge them and then deliberately choose to redirect your mental energy. Some people find it helpful to have a physical cue—touching a meaningful object, taking three deep breaths, or simply saying "reset" out loud.

This is about systematically preparing your mind to recognize and act on opportunities when they appear. The brain that's been rehearsing success is simply better equipped to create it.

The three-year-old standing at the top of the BMX bowl didn't pause to consider the physics of what he was about to attempt. He didn't calculate the angle of descent or weigh the probability of success against the potential for spectacular failure. He just looked down at the concrete curve that dropped away beneath his feet, gripped his tiny handlebars, and pushed off.

My son sailed down that bowl with the kind of fearless commitment that made every parent in the vicinity simultaneously gasp and reach for their phones to capture the moment. While twelve-year-old kids stood at the rim, hesitating and second-guessing, this toddler treated it like the most natural thing in the world. He acted as if success was simply the expected outcome.

Watching him, I felt that familiar mix of pride and terror that comes with parenting, but also something else: recognition. I was witnessing belief in its purest form, unclouded by experience, unfiltered by the accumulated wisdom of past failures. My son possessed something I'd spent years trying to reclaim in my own life: the ability to act as if positive outcomes were inevitable.

We're all born with this capacity. But somewhere along the way, we learn to think ourselves out of our own commitments. We call it "insight." Usually it's just fear dressed up as wisdom. We start cataloging all the ways things could go wrong, all the reasons why our dreams might be unrealistic, all the evidence that we should probably aim lower.

This is why belief stands apart from all the other commitment tools we've explored. You can have the most sophisticated tracking systems, the most supportive mentors, the most carefully designed environments, but without the foundational belief that your efforts will eventually pay off, those tools become elaborate exercises in putting on an act.

Think about it: Why would you meticulously track your progress if you believed that progress was impossible? Why would you seek out mentors if you believed their guidance was pointless? Why would you design your environment to support your goals if you believed those goals were fantasy?

Belief is what transforms all those practical tools from mere activities into investments in a future you can actually envision. It's what makes the difference between going through the motions and genuinely committing to the process of change.

What I've learned from watching my son—and from my own journey through the peaks and valleys of professional athletics—is that belief is something we need to remember rather than manufacture from scratch. That three-year-old fearlessness remains buried under years of accumulated caution and self-protection.

The mental rehearsal techniques that Shawn learned in gymnastics, the visualization practices that helped me navigate high-pressure moments in the NFL, the systematic approach to managing doubt that we've both developed in our business ventures—these are sophisticated ways of accessing something we once knew instinctively.

Every commitment worth making requires us to act before we have proof that our efforts will succeed. That's the nature of commitment itself—moving forward despite uncertainty. And belief—the trained, disciplined, practiced kind—is what makes that movement possible.

Watching my son navigate that BMX track, I was reminded that believing in unlikely outcomes is the most practical thing you can do. Because in a world where so many people hesitate at the edge of their own potential, the simple act of maintaining belief in what's possible becomes a competitive advantage.

Somewhere inside, the three-year-old is still ready to push off. The work is learning to hear him again.

BELIEF IS TRAINABLE. Mental rehearsal creates the same neural pathways as physical practice. Your brain literally rewires for success through visualization.

MENTAL REPS ARE HARDER THAN PHYSICAL ONES. Visualizing five perfect performances while sitting motionless requires more discipline than any workout. Shawn's pre-competition routine demanded as much focus as the routines themselves.

YOUR MIND WILL FILL UNCERTAINTY WITH SOMETHING. Every commitment involves unknowns. You're rehearsing either success scenarios or disaster scenarios. Choose deliberately.

INTERRUPT CATASTROPHIC THINKING. When doubt creeps into visualization, stop and start over. Complete clean mental reps the way you'd complete clean physical ones.

BUILD EVIDENCE FILES. Collect stories of others who've succeeded, your own past wins, the small progress you've

already made. Pull these out when belief
wavers.

FEARLESSNESS IS NATIVE. That three-
year-old confidence remains buried under
years of accumulated caution. The BMX
bowl doesn't scare the toddler. Belief can
be recovered.

17

—

Costs

Imagine this: You're fourteen, exhausted from four hours of practice, and you've just face-planted trying to stick a landing for the hundredth time that week. Your hands are raw, your confidence is shot, and suddenly the idea of doing literally anything else with your life seems like paradise. So you march up to your coach, heart pounding, and announce that you want to quit gymnastics.

Most coaches would give you a pep talk. Maybe remind you of your goals or tell you that champions are made in moments like these. My coach, Chow, would just shrug and say, "Great. You're done with practice today. Don't come in tomorrow. Call me and tell me how you feel."

The first time this happened, I was stunned. I'd worked myself up for a big dramatic conversation, maybe even tears, and he just . . . agreed?

Permission to walk away came without negotiation, guilt trip, or reminder of everything we'd worked toward.

"If you still don't want to do gymnastics tomorrow," he'd continue casually, "take the week off. But you need to find something else to replace it. Tell me what that's going to be."

And that was it. He'd turn back to coaching the other girls like I'd just asked about the weather.

The thing is, quitting had never been easy before. I'd imagined having to fight for it, to prove I really meant it, to overcome objections and arguments. But Chow's complete lack of resistance was unnerving. It was like he was calling my bluff before I even knew I was bluffing.

So I'd go home, reveling in my newfound freedom for exactly one day. I'd sleep in, watch TV, imagine all the normal teenage things I could do instead of spending my afternoons upside down on a four-inch beam. It felt luxurious.

By day two, though, something strange would happen. I'd start thinking about what I actually wanted to do instead. Chow had been clear: I needed to find a replacement activity. So I'd look into track and field, or cheerleading, or dance. I'd check practice schedules and requirements. I'd imagine starting over with a new coach who didn't know me, new teammates who'd already formed their bonds, new skills I'd have to build from scratch.

The fantasy would start to curdle.

I'd think about the thousands of hours I'd already invested in gymnastics—the physical training, yes, but also learning to read Chow's corrections, understanding the rhythm of our gym, building relationships with teammates who'd become like sisters. I'd remember that I actually loved the feeling of nailing a routine, the rush of conquering something that had seemed impossible just weeks before.

By the time I called Chow, usually within forty-eight hours, I'd have a strange new clarity. "I want to come back," I'd tell him.

"Okay," he'd say simply. "See you at practice."

No questions about my change of heart, no requirement that I grovel or promise never to doubt again. He'd welcome me back like I'd never left, and somehow the gym would feel like home in a way it hadn't before my brief exodus.

This happened three times during my career. Three separate moments when I was convinced I was done, when the costs of staying felt impossibly high. But each time, Chow's strategy forced me to confront something I hadn't considered: the costs of leaving.

He forced me to think about everything I'd have to rebuild somewhere else. The trust, the muscle memory, the intricate understanding of how my body moved through space. The relationships, the inside jokes, the shared language of our sport. The identity I'd spent years constructing, one routine at a time.

What Chow understood, and what I'm only now beginning to articulate, is that we're remarkably good at calculating the price of staying put but terrible at tallying the cost of starting over. We see our current struggles in high definition while viewing our alternatives through rose-colored glasses. We forget that every new beginning comes with its own start-up costs—and those costs are almost always higher than we imagine.

This chapter is about developing a more sophisticated relationship with cost—the financial kind, yes, but also the emotional, relational, and psychological investments that make our commitments valuable. It's about learning to extend your runway instead of jumping from plane to plane. And it's about recognizing that sometimes the most economical choice isn't the one that promises something new, but the one that honors what you've already built.

The truth is, we've all been terrible accountants when it comes to our own lives.

We meticulously compare prices when buying a car, agonizing over interest rates and resale values. We'll drive across town to save five dollars on groceries. But when it comes to the investments we've made in our relationships, careers, and personal growth? We treat them like loose change.

Consider the hidden ledger of a five-year relationship. There's the obvious stuff: the shared lease, the merged friend groups, the inside jokes that would make no sense to anyone else. But dig deeper and you'll find a more complex economy. You've learned each other's love languages through trial and error. You've developed systems for handling conflict that actually work. You've weathered storms together and built trust through a thousand small moments of showing up. Your partner knows exactly how you like your coffee and that you get cranky when you're hungry, while you've mastered the art of knowing when they need space versus when they need reassurance.

Now imagine explaining all this to someone new. Imagine rebuilding that entire infrastructure from scratch—the communication patterns, the shared rhythms, the deep familiarity that comes only from time. The start-up costs are staggering, yet we rarely factor them into our relationship math.

The same blindness afflicts our professional lives. We'll complain about a job that's hit a rough patch, fantasizing about the perfect position elsewhere. We conveniently forget about the three years it took to understand our current office's unspoken rules, to build credibility with our colleagues, to learn which battles are worth fighting and which hills aren't worth dying on. We've accumulated political capital, developed a reputation, figured out how to get things done despite the bureaucracy. All of that evaporates the moment we badge out for the last time.

Even our hobbies aren't immune to this cost-blindness. Take learning an instrument. The first few months are brutal—your fingers hurt, nothing sounds like music, and every practice session feels like controlled torture. It's tempting to quit and try something easier, something that promises quicker gratification. What we miss is the compound interest of persistence. Those calluses on your fingertips? They're investments that will pay dividends for years. The muscle memory you're painstakingly building, the ear you're slowly training, the confidence you're developing note by note—none of that transfers to your next hobby.

The most committed people understand something the rest of us miss: Maintenance costs are almost always lower than start-up costs. They've learned to distinguish between the productive friction of growth and the destructive friction of futility. And they've developed strategies for making smart decisions about when to double down and when to cut their losses—decisions based on the full cost of both staying and going.

This isn't just anecdotal wisdom—researchers have actually quantified our talent for terrible cost accounting, and the results are both illuminating and slightly embarrassing. Though maybe not in the way economists think.

Back in 1985, psychologists Hal Arkes and Catherine Blumer decided to test our relationship with money and decision-making in the most delightfully cruel way possible. They presented people with this scenario: Imagine you've spent $100 on a ticket for a weekend ski trip to Michigan. Several weeks later, you buy a $50 ticket for a weekend ski trip to Wisconsin. You think you'll enjoy the Wisconsin trip more than the Michigan trip. But as you're putting your Wisconsin ticket in your wallet, you realize both trips are scheduled for the same weekend. The tickets are nonrefundable and nontransferable.

You must choose one. Which do you pick?

According to traditional economic theory, this should be a no-brainer. The $150 you've spent is gone regardless of which trip you choose. Logic dictates you should pick the trip you'll enjoy more—Wisconsin. Case closed.

Only 46 percent of people chose the more enjoyable Wisconsin trip. The majority—54 percent—chose Michigan, the trip that cost twice as much but would bring them less pleasure. Economists looked at this result and declared it proof of human irrationality. Here were people literally choosing to have a worse time just because they couldn't let go of sunk costs.

Think about what choosing Wisconsin actually entails. Sure, you'll enjoy the slopes more, but you're also choosing to completely write off a $100 investment. You're signaling to yourself that your commitments are negotiable, that when something better comes along, you'll abandon what you've already built. You're training yourself to be a quitter.

The researchers didn't stop there. When they offered people free ski trips—removing the sunk-cost element entirely—the distribution split almost evenly: Forty-four percent of people chose the higher-valued Michigan trip and 42 percent chose Wisconsin. Without skin in the game, people made decisions based on the value they thought they'd get. When they had something invested, they honored that investment.

In another experiment, Arkes and Blumer ran a field study at Ohio University's theater. They sold season tickets at three different price points: full price ($15 per ticket), a $2 discount, and a $7 discount. Then they tracked actual attendance. People who paid full price attended an average of 4.11 shows during the first half of the season, while those with discounts attended only 3.32 and 3.29 shows, respectively.

Economists saw this as more evidence of irrational behavior—people forcing themselves to attend shows they didn't really want to see. There's another way to read this data: The people who paid more got more value from their investment. They discovered plays they might have skipped, met people they wouldn't have encountered, had experiences they would have missed if they'd made decisions based purely on momentary inclination.

This is the hidden wisdom of honoring sunk costs: It's about the person you become when you stick with your choices.

I didn't know any of this research when I was deciding whether to quit football. But looking back, I was doing my own version of the ski trip experiment—and I almost chose Wisconsin.

We've already spent a lot of time unpacking the missteps I made: how I tried to protect myself from the pain of getting released; how I let distractions blur my focus. But eventually, through a lot of trial and error and a realization that there was an inevitable sunset to this opportunity, I finally started remembering what it meant to really commit again to football, to block out the noise and stay focused.

Picture this: My phone buzzes with a text that should have made me jump for joy. It's from a company offering me what could only be described as a dream job: angel investing, working with start-ups, everything I thought I wanted to do after football. The salary was more than respectable, the work was intellectually stimulating, and frankly, it felt like a sign from the universe that maybe it was time to hang up my cleats and move on to something more stable.

It would have made all the sense in the world for me to say yes immediately. The writing was on the wall: I'd been cut nine times by different NFL franchises. I was clearly not the football player I thought I was. Here was a golden parachute, a chance to pivot into a prestigious career that didn't involve getting tackled by 250-pound linebackers or waking up at 5 a.m. to practice snapping footballs through goalposts.

But I couldn't do it.

When I told people about turning down the job, they looked at me like I'd lost my mind. My friends were asking if I'd suffered one too many concussions. And the logical part of my brain was screaming that they were all right—that I was falling victim to the sunk-cost fallacy, throwing good years after bad just because I couldn't admit that my football dreams were over.

But here's what everyone missed, including the rational part of my brain: Walking away would have cost me more than staying.

I was giving up on a version of myself I'd been building for over a decade, when signals and experts were telling me there might still be a chance. Every morning I'd spent in the weight room since high school, every time I'd chosen film study over social time, every sacrifice I'd made to get faster, stronger, more precise—all of that would become a dead-end story. The kid who'd dreamed of playing on Sundays would officially become the guy who almost made it.

More importantly, taking that job would have taught me something dangerous about myself: that when things got difficult, when the path wasn't linear, when success wasn't guaranteed, I was the kind of person who took the easy exit. I would have learned that my commitments were conditional, that they expired the moment a better option appeared.

So I did something that looked completely irrational from the outside: I extended my runway. Instead of jumping ship, I gave myself more time to see if this football thing could work out. I turned down guaranteed money for the possibility of maybe, possibly, making a roster somewhere.

The beautiful irony is that staying created space for something better to emerge. I started taking feedback more seriously, adjusting my training, saying yes to every tryout, while being more strategic about which teams I pursued.

When I finally made it back onto an NFL roster, it was because I'd become the kind of person who doesn't quit when things get hard. That mindset has served me in everything since—marriage, business, parenting. The discipline of honoring my investment in football taught me how to honor investments in general.

Looking back, that venture capital job was like the Wisconsin ski trip—objectively more enjoyable in the short term, but a betrayal of everything I'd already invested in becoming. The real cost was the person I would have become if I'd learned that quitting was always an option.

But how do you know when you're making a wise investment versus throwing good money after bad? The key is learning to ask better questions about costs—the obvious ones that show up on spreadsheets, yes, but also the hidden expenses that become visible only when you know where to look.

The right questions can reveal what you stand to gain by staying the course, and what you might be unconsciously paying by constantly starting from the beginning. Here's how to audit the true economics of your commitments:

WHAT ARE YOUR TRUE SUNK COSTS?

Most people think sunk costs are just about money, but the deepest investments are often invisible. There's the trust you've built over years of showing up consistently. The generational relationships you and your family have in your hometown. The institutional knowledge you've accumulated about how things really work. The calluses—literal or metaphorical—that let you handle what would break a beginner. The reputation that precedes you and opens doors before you even walk into a room. These aren't line items on a balance sheet, but they're often your most valuable assets. Before you walk away, ask yourself: What am I really giving up that I can't put a price tag on?

WHAT ARE THE COMPOUND COSTS OF STARTING OVER?

Every fresh start comes with an invisible reset button that erases more than you think. There's the time tax of climbing learning curves you've already conquered. The emotional cost of feeling incompetent after years of mastery. The relationship overhead of proving yourself to new people who don't yet know your capabilities. The decision fatigue of navigating unfamiliar systems and unspoken rules. Add it up honestly: How much of your life energy will be consumed by simply getting back to where you already are?

WHAT'S THE OPPORTUNITY COST OF YOUR CURRENT FRUSTRATION?

When something feels hard or stuck, it's tempting to assume the grass is greener elsewhere. Difficulty often signals proximity to breakthrough rather than failure. Are you frustrated because you're genuinely in the wrong place, or because you're in the uncomfortable zone where real growth happens? Sometimes the highest opportunity cost is abandoning something right before it pays off. Consider: What might you discover about yourself and your capabilities if you stay long enough to get really good at this?

HOW MUCH WOULD YOU PAY TO GET BACK TO WHERE YOU ARE?

This is the question that cuts through all the noise. If you had to rebuild your current position from scratch—the relationships, the knowledge, the reputation, the skills—what would that actually cost you in time, money, and emotional energy? If someone offered to sell you your exact current situation for that price, would you pay it? Often the answer reveals that what feels like a burden is actually an asset you couldn't afford to repurchase.

WHAT ARE YOU REALLY BUYING WHEN YOU STAY?

Every time you push through when quitting feels easier, you're buying a stronger commitment muscle. Every problem you solve rather than avoid builds your problem-solving portfolio. Every difficult conversation you navigate rather than escape teaches you how to handle the next one. The question isn't just what you've already invested, but what additional capabilities you're purchasing with your continued commitment.

WHAT'S THE IDENTITY COST OF EACH CHOICE?

Perhaps the most expensive cost of all is what each decision teaches you about who you are. Walking away trains you to be someone who quits when things get hard. Staying trains you to be someone who honors commitments even when they're difficult. Both become self-reinforcing patterns that compound over time. Ask yourself: Which version of me am I investing in with this choice? And what will that version of me be capable of five years from now?

WHEN IS IT TIME TO CUT YOUR LOSSES?

Of course, there are times when the wisest economic choice is to walk away—when your commitment is actively harming your health, your relationships, or your future potential. As we explored in chapter 10, some situations are genuinely toxic and require the courage to leave. The key is distinguishing between productive discomfort (the kind that builds strength) and destructive patterns (the kind that diminish you). If you find yourself asking these questions and consistently arriving at answers that point toward damage rather than growth, it may be time to honor your investment by redirecting it somewhere healthier.

The real cost accounting is about understanding the full price tag of both staying and going—the obvious expenses, yes, but also the hidden investments, the compound returns, and the person you become through each choice. When you start asking these deeper questions about costs, you often discover that what looked like throwing good money after bad was actually the smartest investment you could make. And sometimes you realize that the "economical" choice to cut your losses would have cost you everything that truly mattered.

We've applied these questions to our own marriage. When we look at our relationship through an economist's lens, the numbers are frankly terrifying. We've made leaving each other almost impossibly expensive.

Our finances are completely intertwined—what's mine is hers and what's hers is mine. We work together every day, building a business that would be nearly impossible to divide. We have children whose lives would be upended by separation. We've bought a house, planned a future, built friendships as a couple that would become awkward if we split.

From the outside, this might look like we've trapped ourselves. A relationship counselor might warn about staying together "for the kids" or remaining married because divorce would be too costly. We've heard people describe similar situations as being "stuck."

Here's what that analysis misses: Every one of those "costs" is also an investment paying compound interest. The shared business is a daily reminder that we dream together, build together, win or lose as a team. The merged finances mean we talk about everything, negotiate everything, can't make major decisions in isolation. We're genuine partners in every sense.

The children are the ultimate expression of our commitment to something larger than ourselves. When we watch our daughter inherit Andrew's stubborn streak or our son flash Shawn's mischievous smile, we're seeing compound returns on our investment in each other.

Even the house represents more than shared debt. Its walls have heard our arguments and our laughter; the kitchen has seen thousands of meals. The mortgage is a commitment device that forces us to solve problems rather than run from them.

We didn't engineer these entanglements strategically. They evolved naturally as we kept choosing each other, day after day, year after year. Each shared investment made the next one easier, until leaving would require dismantling an entire life.

And here's what we've learned: Marriage, when rooted in commitment, holds you long enough to get to the end of yourself. It gives you space to let old dreams die and stay in the room long enough to discover what comes next. In relationships without this structure, people walk away when expectations collapse. Marriage keeps you around long enough to realize that the death of a dream isn't the end. It's the end of a small dream. There's still so much left.

The real economics of love reveal themselves in accumulated dividends: shorthand conversations that convey novels of meaning, reflexive trust that eliminates constant negotiation, shared dreams that become more vivid with each passing year. These returns compound only when you resist the temptation to liquidate at the first sign of turbulence.

Understanding the true cost of commitment changes how we approach difficult seasons. When you count what you're still earning, walking away becomes almost unimaginable. The question shifts from "Can I afford to stay?" to "Can I afford to start over?"

And the answer, more often than not, is that you were already home—you just needed forty-eight hours to realize it.

WE'RE TERRIBLE ACCOUNTANTS OF OUR OWN LIVES. We'll drive across town to save five dollars on groceries but abandon years of relationship building over temporary friction.

MAINTENANCE BEATS REBUILDING. Reconstructing trust, skills, and reputation from scratch almost always cost more than working through current problems.

THE REAL SUNK COSTS ARE INVISIBLE. Muscle memory, institutional knowledge, inside jokes, the identity you've spent years constructing. None of these transfer to your next venture.

ASK THE BILLION-DOLLAR QUESTION. If you had to rebuild your current position from scratch, what would you pay for it? Often the answer reveals that your "burden" is actually an asset.

COMMITMENT COMPOUNDS. Each shared investment adds mass to your relationship, career, or calling. The

dividends of persistence only pay off
when you resist liquidating at the first sign
of turbulence.

KNOW WHEN TO WALK AWAY. Some
commitments genuinely harm your health,
relationships, or future potential. The key is
distinguishing productive discomfort from
destructive patterns.

18

Grace

We've spent the better part of this book convincing you to stick with things when they get hard. We've told you to design environments that make quitting inconvenient, to announce your goals publicly, to measure everything that moves. We've essentially turned you into a commitment-seeking missile, armed with metrics and accountability partners.

And now we're going to tell you something that might sound contradictory: Be nice to yourself.

We know, we know. After seventeen chapters of "buckle down and push through," suggesting self-compassion feels a bit like telling someone to floor the gas pedal and pump the brakes simultaneously. But here's the thing we've learned from our own spectacular failures at sticking with things: The voice in your head can either be your greatest ally or your most creative saboteur.

Most of us have mastered the art of being our own worst boss. You know the type—the micromanager who nitpicks every mistake, never acknowledges progress, and somehow believes that psychological warfare is a management strategy. If you had a friend who talked to you the way you talk to yourself when you mess up a commitment, you'd stage an intervention. Or at least stop returning their calls.

We've all done this dance. You miss one workout and suddenly you're "someone who doesn't exercise." You skip one day of writing and you're "not really a writer." You have one difficult conversation with your spouse and you're "bad at marriage." It's as if we believe that the path to becoming better people runs directly through the Valley of Self-Loathing, and the only way out is to berate ourselves into submission.

Here's what actually happens when we adopt this charming approach: We quit. Not dramatically— that would be too honest. Instead, we engage in what scientists call "self-handicapping," which is a fancy term for the incredibly creative ways we sabotage ourselves while maintaining plausible deniability. We become forensic accountants of our own excuses, finding elaborate reasons why this particular attempt doesn't count, why we'll definitely start fresh next Monday, why the alignment of our schedule and the moon's phases just isn't quite right this time.

The irony is almost poetic: In our quest to hold ourselves accountable, we become the very person we're trying to escape—someone who can't stick with anything.

Grace, it turns out, is the secret weapon of those who've figured out how to stay in the game long enough for commitment to work its magic. It creates the emotional conditions that allow you to keep trying when things get difficult, to learn from mistakes without being crushed by them, and to maintain the kind of long-term perspective that real change requires. When you treat yourself as someone worth believing in, you start acting like someone worth believing in.

The most committed people have learned to handle stumbles with grace, understanding that self-compassion is wisdom, and discovering that being kind to yourself is actually the most practical thing you can do.

I have fallen more times than a person should reasonably fall in one lifetime. I'm not speaking metaphorically. I mean literal, physical, gravity-wins-again falling. By rough calculation, I hit the mat somewhere north of fifty thousand times during my gymnastics career. Falls off the beam deserve their own statistical category.

If you've never done gymnastics, let me paint

you a picture of what all that falling looks like. First, you spend weeks trying to understand what your coach is asking your body to do. Then you spend more weeks attempting the skill and failing so spectacularly that onlookers wonder if you have the faintest idea what you're doing. You land on your back, your stomach, your side—basically every part of your body except your feet. You develop a personal relationship with ice packs. And then, one magical day, you stick the landing. Once. The next day, you're back to falling.

This is where most people would reasonably conclude they're terrible at gymnastics and should take up a less physics-defying hobby. But here's what I learned instead: Gymnastics has the most beautiful relationship with failure of any sport I know. Every fall is information. Every bruise is proof you're trying something difficult.

My coach, Chow, is the one who taught me to see it this way. When I'd attempt a new skill and land flat on my back, he wouldn't rush over with sympathy or launch into corrections. He'd simply say, "Good. Now you know what that feels like. Let's try again." There was something almost cheerful about it. He took my training incredibly seriously, but falls were just part of the curriculum. Pain was tuition. Frustration was the price of admission. And pride was what we earned.

That reframe changed everything. When failure becomes expected, it loses its power to devastate you. When falling is just part of the process, you can get back up with your dignity intact. I remember telling myself a simple phrase during those endless repetitions: "I'm getting one rep closer." Whether I stuck the landing or face-planted, I was accumulating valuable information. The falls were investments.

This mindset followed me out of the gym. When Andrew was struggling through his NFL journey, beating himself up after every disappointment, I found myself channeling Chow. "Nothing is wasted," I'd tell him. "Even this has something to teach you."

It sounds annoyingly optimistic, I know. But this is what grace actually looks like in practice: treating yourself like someone worth believing in. Grace lets you reframe a setback without losing sight of the bigger mission. It keeps you rooted in purpose instead of spiraling into self-judgment. Without it, you start white-knuckling toward your goals, gripping so tightly you sabotage the very thing you're protecting.

I think about this now, watching our daughter learn gymnastics. She gets frustrated when she can't immediately master a cartwheel, and I want to tell her what I wish someone had told me earlier: The goal is to fall better.

There's a particular exhaustion that comes from constantly judging your own performance, treating every mistake as evidence of fundamental inadequacy. Grace gave me permission to be bad at things while getting good at them. It let me see failures as plot points in a larger story rather than final verdicts on my character. Self-compassion, it turns out, is rocket fuel for people who want to keep trying.

After fifty thousand falls, here's what I know: The people who stick with difficult things are the ones who've learned to fail gracefully. They treat setbacks as information rather than identity. They get back up because they've figured out how to be kind to themselves in the process.

Sometimes the most radical thing you can do is decide you're worth believing in, bruises and all.

If Shawn's story sounds like it's just about having a positive attitude, the science suggests otherwise: Grace is a measurable psychological intervention with results that would make any performance coach jealous.

Dr. Kristin Neff, who has spent the better part of two decades studying self-compassion, defines it as treating yourself with the same kindness you'd show a good friend who was struggling. When she puts people through self-compassion training and measures the results, they perform better, stick with difficult tasks longer, and recover from setbacks faster.

In one particularly telling study, Neff and her colleagues had people recall a recent failure or mistake that still made them feel bad. Half the participants were asked to write about this experience with self-compassion—acknowledging their pain, recognizing that failure is part of the human experience, and treating themselves with kindness. The other half were left to stew in their usual self-critical thoughts.

The results were striking. The self-compassion group was significantly more motivated to improve and more likely to tackle similar challenges in the future. The self-criticism group showed all the hallmarks of what psychologists call "learned helplessness"—that defeated, why-bother attitude that makes people give up before they've really tried.

Here's where it gets really interesting for those of us obsessed with commitment: Self-compassion appears to make people more willing to take responsibility for their mistakes. When you're free from defending your ego against your inner critic, you can actually look clearly at what went wrong and figure out how to do better next time.

Juliana Breines and Serena Chen at UC Berkeley demonstrated this beautifully. In their study, people took a difficult test, failed it, and then had the opportunity to study for a retest. Those who were coached to respond to their failure with self-compassion spent significantly more time studying for the second test. The self-critical group avoided preparation altogether, as if looking at their mistakes was too painful to bear.

You see this pattern everywhere once you start

looking for it. The people who bounce back from divorce grieve, learn, and eventually try again. The entrepreneurs who build successful companies after their first start-up tanks can look honestly at what went wrong without making it mean they're fundamentally flawed human beings.

This research helps explain something that long puzzled us: why some people seem to get stronger from failure while others get crushed by it. Resilient people have learned to process these experiences differently. They've figured out how to be simultaneously honest about their shortcomings and compassionate about their humanity.

The most successful people have mastered what researchers call "emotional regulation." They can feel disappointed without becoming devastated, frustrated without becoming furious at themselves, and confused without concluding they're irredeemably stupid.

Think about it this way: If you had a friend who was trying to learn piano, and they came to you after missing a week of practice, what would you say? Probably something like "That happens to everyone. What matters is getting back to it now." You certainly wouldn't launch into a lecture about their fundamental lack of discipline.

Yet when we miss our own week of practice—whether it's exercise, writing, meditation, or calling our parents—we somehow think the appropriate response is to become our own worst enemy. We've confused self-improvement with self-punishment, as if suffering were a prerequisite for growth.

The research suggests we've got it exactly backward. Grace makes high standards sustainable over time. Understanding the theory is one thing. Living it is another. Let Andrew tell you about the difference between knowing grace matters and actually practicing it when your world is falling apart.

I used to think grace was what happened after you succeeded—a kind of victory lap for people who had already figured everything out. Then I got cut from the Kansas City Chiefs, and I discovered that grace is actually what you need most when you're sitting in your car in a parking lot, wondering if your dreams just died.

Picture this: You're twenty-four years old, you've worked your entire life for one thing, and a coach you've never met before just told you that your services are no longer required. Thank you for your time, good luck in your future endeavors, security will escort you out. It's the kind of moment that makes you question everything—your talent, your work ethic, your fundamental understanding of how the universe works.

My immediate response was to become a

one-man symposium on my own inadequacy. I replayed every practice, every snap, every inter-action with coaches, searching for the fatal flaw that explained my failure. I was like a detective investigating my own incompetence, and business was booming.

This is where Shawn came in, armed with what I now recognize as a PhD in applied grace.

While I was busy constructing an elaborate case for why I was clearly terrible at football and probably life in general, she was doing something completely different. She was looking for what she called "the gifts in the mess." Not in some saccha-rine, everything-happens-for-a-reason way, but with genuine curiosity about what good might emerge from what felt like a disaster.

"You know," she said one evening, "if you hadn't gone to Kansas City, we never would have met Cairo and Dustin." She was talking about my teammates who had become genuine friends. "And you never would have learned how to handle that kind of pressure. And you definitely wouldn't have those stories that make me laugh until I cry."

I wanted to argue with her. I wanted to point out that friendship and funny stories were poor consolation prizes for a dead dream. But some-thing about the way she said it made me pause. She wasn't minimizing my disappointment or try-ing to talk me out of feeling bad. She was simply offering a different lens through which to view the same events.

This became our pattern. I would catastroph- ize; she would redirect. Not to a fantasy where everything was perfect, but to a more complete picture of what was actually happening. When I focused exclusively on what I'd lost, she'd gently point toward what I'd gained. When I treated each setback as evidence of my fundamental unworthi- ness, she'd treat it as information about what to try next.

The crazy thing is, her approach actually made me more honest about my failures, not less. When someone believes you're capable of learning and growing, you stop spending so much energy defending yourself and start spending more energy actually learning and growing.

I remember one particularly low moment when I'd been cut from yet another team. I was lying on our couch, dramatically declaring that I was obviously not meant to play professional football and should probably just give up and get a normal job. Shawn listened to my whole speech, nodded thoughtfully, and then said, "Okay, but before you retire, can you at least call back that coach from Seattle who left you three voicemails?"

She had this way of acknowledging my feelings without getting trapped in my stories. Yes, getting cut sucked. Yes, it was disappointing and frustrat- ing and genuinely difficult. And also: It was one chapter, not the whole book.

Looking back, I realize Shawn was teaching me something researchers have since quantified:

Self-compassion creates the emotional conditions that allow you to keep trying when things get hard. She modeled a way of being disappointed without being devastated, frustrated without being furious, honest about setbacks without letting them define me. She held the difficulty and the perspective at the same time.

The beautiful irony: By refusing to let me beat myself up, she made me more willing to take risks, more open to feedback, more resilient. Grace, it turns out, is what allows you to handle the truth without it destroying you.

Sometimes we need someone else to teach us how to be kind to ourselves. But what if you don't have your own personal Shawn? What if the people around you are just as committed to catastrophizing as you are? The good news is that grace, like any other skill, can be learned. Here are the practices that have worked for us and the people we've learned from.

START WITH THE FRIEND TEST

The next time you mess up a commitment, ask yourself a simple question: What would I say to a good friend in this exact situation? Then say that to yourself instead. It sounds almost embarrassingly simple, but there's something powerful about stepping outside your own drama and accessing the wisdom you'd naturally offer someone else. You already know how to be compassionate; you just need to turn that skill inward.

ZOOM OUT

When you're stuck in the immediate sting of a setback, deliberately shift your perspective. Imagine yourself five years from now, looking back on this moment. What would that future version of yourself want you to know? Often, what feels catastrophic today becomes a footnote in a larger story of growth.

Andrew discovered this through his journaling practice—he's kept a running Google Doc of his thoughts since 2009. When he was struggling through NFL disappointments, he'd go back and read entries from years earlier. Suddenly, problems that had once felt insurmountable seemed almost quaint. The eighteen-year-old Andrew who was thrilled just to get a call from a college coach would have been amazed by the twenty-four-year-old Andrew who was beating himself up for not being signed by a professional team. Reading his past struggles reminded him how temporary most problems really are.

CREATE GRACE RITUALS

We introduced the Five-Minute Journal to our routine, which asks simple questions that force you to notice what's going right. Instead of asking what went wrong today, it prompts you to identify three things you're grateful for and three things that would make tomorrow great. It sounds almost annoyingly simple, but there's something powerful about training your brain to scan for positives rather than problems.

At our office, we've institutionalized this with something we call "the Famies"—impromptu award ceremonies where we celebrate small victories with a bobblehead trophy (admittedly chewed up by our one-year-old), confetti poppers, and genuine applause for things like a successful project launch, no matter how small.

There's power in marking moments that would otherwise disappear into the blur of daily work. Grace grows when you have evidence that you're capable of more than your worst moments suggest. Your brain needs data to counter its natural negativity bias.

REFRAME YOUR LANGUAGE

Notice the difference between "I'm terrible at this" and "I'm learning this." Between "I always fail" and "This didn't work this time." These are fundamentally different stories about who you are and what's possible. The first story ends in abandonment; the second invites you to keep going.

EXTEND YOUR TIMELINE

Most self-criticism comes from expecting immediate results from long-term processes. Remind yourself regularly that meaningful change happens on geological time, not social media time. The person trying to lose weight who gains a pound this week isn't failing—they're participating in a months-long process that includes natural fluctuations.

FIND YOUR GRACE PARTNERS

Andrew was lucky—he married someone who naturally practiced grace. You can deliberately cultivate relationships with people who see your potential even when you can't. Tell a trusted friend or family member that you're working on being kinder to yourself and ask them to help redirect you when you start spiraling. Sometimes the most powerful thing someone can do is simply say, "You're being way too hard on yourself right now."

These practices work because they gradually shift the relationship you have with yourself from adversarial to collaborative. Instead of fighting against your own humanity, you learn to work with it. You stop expecting perfection and start expecting progress. And in that shift, the very qualities that make you human—your capacity for growth, learning, and resilience—become your greatest assets in keeping the commitments that matter most.

Grace changes the entire game, turning commitment from an exercise in willpower into an act of self-respect. When you treat yourself as someone worth investing in, commitment stops feeling like punishment and starts feeling like the most natural thing in the world—because of course you'd show up for someone you believe in. Of course you'd keep trying for someone whose potential you can see. That someone is you. It always was.

CHAPTER 18 SUMMARY

SELF-COMPASSION IS ROCKET FUEL. People who practice it stick with difficult tasks longer, recover from setbacks faster, and are more motivated to improve after failures. The research is unambiguous.

WE'VE CONFUSED IMPROVEMENT WITH PUNISHMENT. Most people have mastered being their own worst boss: the micromanager who believes psychological warfare is a management strategy.

THE FRIEND TEST WORKS. Ask yourself what you'd say to a good friend in your exact situation. Then say that to yourself instead. You already know how to be compassionate. Turn the skill inward.

GRACE MAKES HIGH STANDARDS SUSTAINABLE. When failure becomes expected rather than exceptional, it loses its power to devastate you. Setbacks become information rather than identity.

LANGUAGE SHAPES STORY. "I'm learning this" invites you to keep going. "I'm terrible at this" ends in abandonment. The frame determines the trajectory.

FIND YOUR GRACE PARTNERS. Cultivate relationships with people who see your potential even when you can't. Shawn did this for Andrew through every NFL disappointment. Sometimes you need someone else to believe in you until you can believe in yourself.

The Beginning

So here we are, two-hundred-odd pages later. Endings have never been our strong suit. Just ask anyone who's watched us leave a dinner party. We say goodbye seventeen times and somehow end up staying another hour discussing the host's espresso machine. Which, now that we think about it, is the perfect metaphor for commitment: Even our exits involve accidental reinvestment.

Here's what we hope you've gathered from this journey: Commitment is choosing to stay in the room with something—or someone—long enough to discover what's actually possible.

That's it. That's the whole secret.

We've talked with so many people who thought they were missing some essential commitment gene. They'd describe abandoned gym memberships, half-finished novels, relationships that never made it past the three-month mark. But after hundreds of conversations, thousands of hours of practice, and more athletic face-plants than any reasonable humans should endure, we've come to believe something different. People struggle with commitment because nobody told them it's a learnable skill. And nobody told them it doesn't feel the way they expect it to.

Commitment rarely feels like the movies promised it would. If that were true, Olympic athletes would never have bad training days, successful marriages would never involve arguments about laundry, and nobody would write a book while wanting to throw their laptop out the window.

Real commitment feels like showing up to practice when you'd rather be anywhere else. It feels like having the same conversation with your spouse for the fifteenth time and still trying to understand each other. It feels like sitting down to write when the words come out like they've been through a blender.

Commitment often feels boring. And difficult. And thankless. That's how you know it's working. All the tools we've shared—the metrics, mentors, environment design, belief training—are really elaborate ways to help you do one simple thing: stay in the room when leaving would be easier.

Because here's what happens when you stay: You get to watch the magic unfold in slow motion. The relationship that felt stuck breaks through to new depth. The skill that seemed impossible becomes second nature. The creative project that felt like garbage transforms into something you're proud of. The business that almost failed five times becomes the thing that changes your life.

None of that happens on a timeline you can predict or control. Commitment asks you to show up without knowing when the payoff will come, or what form it will take. It's like planting a garden in the dark and watering it faithfully, trusting that something's happening underground even when you can't see the surface.

This is why we called this conclusion "The Beginning." Because the end of this book is the opening to decide what to do with everything we've shared. And despite having just written an entire book on what we've learned about the power of commitment, we need to be honest about something: You might not be ready.

That's okay. Genuinely.

Maybe you picked up this book because someone who loves you thought you needed it. Maybe you're in a phase of life where keeping your options open genuinely serves you better than narrowing your focus. Maybe you need to do more exploring before you're ready to choose something—or someone—to pour yourself into fully.

Commitment isn't universally good. Committing

to the wrong things can be just as problematic as committing to nothing. We've seen people stay in relationships that were actively harmful because they thought commitment meant never walking away. We've watched friends pour years into careers that made them miserable because they'd already "invested so much." We've done it ourselves, too—hung on too long to things that needed to end because we confused commitment with stubbornness.

So if you're not ready to commit to something big right now, please don't.

Instead, maybe start small. Really small. Embarrassingly small. That's why we spent so much time on small commitments. Because that's where most of us need to begin: with the radical act of doing what we said we'd do, even when it's inconvenient.

Call your mom once a week. Read for ten minutes before bed. Water that plant that's somehow still clinging to life despite your best efforts to neglect it. These aren't the commitments that make for inspiring TED Talks, but they're the ones that teach your brain you're someone who follows through.

Because here's another thing we've learned: Commitment compounds. The person who masters small commitments develops the capacity for larger ones. The couple that figures out how to stay connected through the infant years builds the skills to navigate the teenage years. The entrepreneur who sees one small project through to completion develops the stomach for bigger risks.

You don't have to revolutionize your life tomorrow. You just have to choose one thing—one small, specific thing—and practice showing up for it even when showing up feels hard.

This is what we hope for you—not that you'll finish this book and immediately commit to something huge and life-changing (though if you do, please email us because we love a good story), but that you'll start to see yourself as someone capable of committing. Someone who understands that the most interesting parts of life often happen after the initial excitement wears off.

We also hope you'll be gentle with yourself when you inevitably stumble. Because you will stumble. You'll miss workouts and forget to journal and snap at your partner even though you swore you were going to be more patient. You'll abandon projects and break promises to yourself and wonder if you're just destined to be someone who can't stick with anything.

When that happens—and it will happen—we hope you'll remember what we said about grace. We hope you'll treat yourself like a good friend who's trying something difficult. We hope you'll get back up not because you're stronger than everyone else, but because you've learned that falling is just part of the curriculum.

Most of all, we hope you'll remember that commitment is about developing a kind of resilient stubbornness, the voice that says, "I'm going to keep showing up and see what happens." You'll waver. You'll doubt. You'll want to quit. That's the process. That's what staying looks like from the inside.

So whatever you're considering committing to—a person, a project, a practice, a dream—we want to leave you with this: You're more capable than you think. Humans are remarkably adaptable creatures who can learn almost anything if they persist.

The path forward isn't complicated. Pick something that matters. Start smaller than you think you should. Show up more consistently than feels reasonable. Be kinder to yourself than seems necessary. And when you want to quit, remember that feeling like quitting and actually quitting are two very different things.

We can't promise it will be easy. We can't promise it will always be fun. We can't even promise it will work out the way you hope. But we can promise this: If you practice the art of commitment, if you learn to find the sacred in the repetitive and the profound in the mundane, your life will be richer for it. Richer in depth. In meaning. In the quiet satisfaction that comes from knowing you're someone who stays.

**With love, stubbornness,
and way too much coffee,
Shawn & Andrew**

P.S. If you made it all the way through this book, you've already proven you can commit to something. See? You're better at this than you thought. Now go forth and stay in some rooms. We'll be cheering for you from ours.

ACKNOWLEDGMENTS

Books about commitment require their own acts of commitment from many people, and we've been fortunate to have a team who stayed in the room with us through every draft, every revision, and every moment when we wondered if we were actually making sense.

Our profound gratitude begins with the editorial team at Portfolio, who saw the promise in our initial ideas and helped us shape them into something worthy of readers' time and attention. Your patience with our athletic metaphors and your gentle suggestions that not everything needs to relate back to gymnastics or football have meant more than you know. So has your unwavering belief that this message matters. Thank you for pushing us to dig deeper when we were tempted to stay on the surface, and for knowing exactly when to say "that story needs to stay" even when we thought it might be too personal.

To Bryan Norman, our literary agent, whose guidance through the mysterious world of publishing has been invaluable. Thank you for fielding our panicked texts, talking us through our doubts, and believing in this book when we needed it most.

To Jimmy Soni, who brought his talent as a writer to this project and helped us transform years of lived experience into words that actually make sense. You took our rambling stories, half-formed insights, and sometimes contradictory thoughts and somehow wove them into a coherent narrative that still sounds like us—only better. Your ability to find the universal truths in our specific experiences, to know when to push us for more detail and when to pull back, and to maintain both warmth and clarity throughout has been nothing short of miraculous. Thank you for your patience with our endless revisions, your good humor about our tendency to relate everything back to sports, and most importantly, for helping us tell our story in a way that might actually help others tell theirs.

To Drew, Jett, and Bear—you three are our greatest teachers in the art of showing up daily. You've shown us that commitment looks different at every age, whether it's a three-year-old's determination to master the BMX bowl or the patience required to help with tying shoes for the thousandth time. You keep us honest about what matters most, and you remind us daily that love is the ultimate commitment. We hope someday you'll read this book and understand why we were always going on about "sticking with things."

To our parents, who modeled commitment long before we had words for it. Dad, your 473-day streak of writing devotionals taught us that consistency creates its own kind of magic. Your morning tandem bike rides turned every commute into an adventure and taught us that metrics can transform the ordinary into something extraordinary. Mom, your quiet dedication to our family showed us that the most important commitments often happen without fanfare. And to Shawn's parents, who worked through the night at multiple jobs and drove countless hours to gymnastics practices and competitions, who never wavered in their support even when the path seemed impossible—your commitment to her dreams made everything else possible.

This book exists because of the coaches and trainers who refused to let us settle for less than our potential. To Coach Liang Chow, whose unique blend of discipline and grace taught a young girl from Iowa that commitment could coexist with joy. Your belief that effort matters more than outcomes shaped not just a gymnast, but an entire approach to life. To James Franklin, who showed a struggling college student that transformation was possible with the right systems and support. Your 4:30 a.m. workouts were brutal, but they built character and resilience that extends far beyond football.

To the mentors who appeared at crucial moments—some for a season, others for a single conversation that redirected our entire trajectory. Uncle Jim, who knew when to push and when to simply believe, who turned an eight-month engagement timeline into twenty-four hours and taught us that sometimes the best moments come from bold action. Jeremy Bloom, whose back-seat challenge to think bigger changed how we approach everything. You taught us that sometimes the greatest gift someone can give is refusing to let you think small.

To our teammates in business and life who've weathered our experiments, endured our enthusiasm for tracking everything, and celebrated the small victories that eventually became big ones. To our online community, who've been with us through pivots and changes, always reminding us why authentic connection matters more than perfect production.

To the readers who shared their own stories of commitment with us—in emails, at events, in passing conversations that stayed with us. You reminded us that everyone has their own version of a double-twisting double back, their own daily practice of showing up when it would be easier not to. Your vulnerability in sharing your struggles and triumphs shaped how we approached writing this book.

To our entire support team—from editors to designers, from early readers to those who offered feedback that made us reconsider and revise—thank you for your commitment to making this book the best version of itself. Your dedication to excellence pushed us to dig deeper and share more honestly than we might have otherwise dared.

Finally, to everyone like us who's ever been told

they "just can't stick with anything"—this book is for you, and because of you. Your struggles inspired us to dig deeper into our own experiences and find something useful to share. Thank you for trusting us with your stories and for being willing to try again.

Writing a book about commitment while managing three young kids, multiple businesses, and all of life's daily demands required its own acts of sustained dedication. It required early mornings and late nights, countless conversations about what really mattered, and more drafts than we care to count. But it also reminded us of everything we believe about the power of staying in the room long enough to see what's possible.

To everyone who stayed in the room with us—thank you.

The East Family Vision Setting Method

Throughout this book, we've shared strategies for maintaining commitments—from tracking metrics to designing supportive environments. But there's one practice we've saved for the end, a method we've refined over years of trial and error that brings everything together: our annual vision setting ritual.

What follows is the actual framework we use each January to reflect on the past year and plan for the next. It's part data analysis, part dreaming session, and part couples therapy (the good kind). We've included it here not as a prescription but as a starting point—a template you can adapt, modify, or completely reimagine based on what works for your own life. The core principle is simple: What gets observed gets altered. By taking time to intentionally review where you've been and thoughtfully plan where you're going, you create the conditions for meaningful progress across all areas of life.

This method has evolved significantly since our first awkward attempt at goal setting as newlyweds. Back then, we sat at our kitchen table with a blank piece of paper, argued about whether "be happier" counted as a specific goal, and ultimately gave up after twenty minutes to order takeout instead. Now it's become one of our most cherished annual traditions—a chance to step back from the daily chaos and ask ourselves: Are we actually building the life we want? The framework that follows represents years of refinement, borrowed wisdom from mentors, and plenty of lessons learned the hard way. We hope it serves you as well as it has served us.

EAST VISION SETTING 2023

To effectively implement the East family method of goal setting, it's essential to understand and embrace its core principle: the Hawthorne effect, which posits that what is observed and focused on tends to change or improve. This specific goal setting approach is based in historical data and anecdotal experience, and then those data points are adjusted to increase things we desire more of and decrease unwanted things. The method involves a structured and reflective process, aimed at setting clear, meaningful goals while acknowledging and appreciating the journey of the past year. Here's how you can apply this method:

PROCESS OVERVIEW:

SET ASIDE TIME: Dedicate 3–4 hours on a chosen date (e.g., 1/5/23) for this activity.

DIVIDE THE SESSION:

- ☐ **Debrief:** Spend 1.5 hours reviewing the past year.
- ☐ **Vision Setting:** Allocate another 1.5 hours to envision and set goals for the upcoming year.

CHOOSE A UNIQUE ENVIRONMENT: Conduct this session in a "foreign space" to foster creativity and open-mindedness.

TIME MANAGEMENT: Limit each section to 5 minutes to maintain focus and efficiency.

GOAL STRUCTURING: Break down goals into three categories:

- ☐ **Goals:** Define what you want to achieve.
- ☐ **Changes:** Identify what you want to change.
- ☐ **Growth:** Determine areas for personal and joint growth.

HARMONIZING VISIONS: If visions differ, discuss the differences to reach a consensus on shared goals.

REFLECT AND PRAY: Conclude the session with a prayer, expressing gratitude for the past year and hope for the year ahead, acknowledging that things may not go as planned.

SUMMARIZE THE EXPERIENCE:

- ☐ **Last Year:** Craft a statement summarizing the previous year's experiences and achievements.
- ☐ **Next Year:** Develop a statement outlining hopes and aspirations for the coming year.

EXAMPLE STATEMENTS:

- 2021 REFLECTION: "We are thankful for the stability and growth in 2020, aiming to build on these foundations in 2021 with more efficiency and less stress."
- 2023 THEME: "Prioritize family and impactful actions in our dealings, charitable contributions, and time management."

DETAILED GOAL PLANNING:

- Expand on specific areas such as family mission statements, traditions, budgeting, and personal development.
- Set concrete goals in various life aspects, including these twelve areas: finances, travel, family activities, friendship, marriage, health, philanthropy, home improvement, faith, business, personal growth, and children's milestones.

IMPLEMENTING THE METHOD:

- Use this structure as a guide, customizing it to fit your family's unique dynamics and aspirations.

- The method emphasizes time-bound, specific goal setting while allowing flexibility and room for unexpected changes.

By following these steps, the East family method provides a well-rounded and reflective approach to goal setting, helping to align individual and shared aspirations within a relationship.

We encourage you to write your goals down, even type them up, so you can easily look back on these next year and decades from now and see how much progress you've made!

The first time you do this will be the longest. You'll need to get acquainted with how to gather the data, how to structure your outlines, how to communicate this together, how to come up with realistic adjustments, etc. But the more you do it, the easier the process becomes.

Every fifth year, we have a "year of jubilee" where we don't refer to historical data, but rather start from scratch to encourage outside-the-box thinking.

PROMPTS

What is the appropriate amount of times you want to check, track, engage in, or do each of the following on average on a monthly basis? Places to look to find this data are Apple Health, Oura Ring, Monarch Money app, photos, etc.

1. Income
2. Expense
3. Giving
4. Investments
5. Church
6. Parents getaway
7. Pray
8. Fast
9. Try new things
10. Local kids activities
11. Take supplement
12. Family dinners
13. Watch kids practice
14. Community groups
15. Date night
16. Read kids books
17. See parents
18. Therapist
19. Home-cooked meals
20. Workout
21. Host
22. Review schedule
23. Hobbies
24. Drink alcohol
25. Family trips
26. Serve
27. Boys/girls nights
28. Eat out
29. Order in
30. Have date night
31. Meet strangers
32. Visit kids' school
33. Drop off kids at school
34. Daddy-daughter dates
35. Catch up with loved ones
36. Read devotionals
37. Do home improvements
38. Meet with mentors
39. Meet with mentees
40. Revisit goals
41. Books read

42. Let people use spare room
43. Attend kids' sports games
44. Gardening
45. Family movie nights
46. Volunteer work
47. Meditation
48. Yoga sessions
49. Family game nights
50. Arts and crafts with kids
51. Attend cultural events
52. Plan future vacations
53. Organize family photos
54. Home organization projects
55. Attend workshops/ seminars
56. Biking as a family
57. Swimming activities
58. Nature walks/ hikes
59. Fishing trips
60. Family music sessions
61. Cooking classes
62. Language learning
63. Teach kids life skills
64. Family health checkups
65. Plan birthday celebrations
66. Attend religious ceremonies
67. Explore new neighborhoods
68. Backyard camping
69. Stargazing nights
70. Maintain a gratitude journal
71. Attend parent-teacher meetings
72. Participate in charity runs/ walks
73. Update family budget
74. Review insurance policies
75. Pet care responsibilities
76. Teach kids about finance
77. Go to the library
78. Start a family book club
79. Attend dance/ music recitals
80. Build something together (DIY)
81. Visit museums
82. Go to the beach
83. Family picnics
84. Attend local festivals
85. Create a family YouTube channel/blog

86. Go to amusement parks

87. Watch educational documentaries

88. Practice musical instruments

89. Plan family reunion events

90. Attend live theater shows

91. Participate in community cleanups

92. Teach kids about recycling

93. Visit elderly relatives

94. Attend sports events

95. Go on historical tours

96. Family bike rides

97. Host sleepovers for kids

98. Go to farmer's markets

99. Attend cooking/ baking workshops

100. Participate in local politics/ community meetings

101. Family fitness challenges

102. Create family vision boards

103. Update wills and estate plans

104. Seasonal home decoration

105. Teach kids about different cultures

106. Attend art exhibitions

107. Plan and execute a family project

108. Discuss current events

109. Go on nature conservation trips

110. Family spa days

111. Learn a new sport together

112. Go fruit picking

113. Plan a surprise for a family member

114. Attend a self-defense class

115. Go on a road trip

116. Watch sunrise/sunset together

117. Start a family business idea

118. Visit an animal shelter

119. Teach kids about environmental conservation

120. Create a family tree/ history project

VISION BOARD

After you finish determining your goals, spend one hour creating a vision board. This is important because, as discussed in the article "Seeing Is Believing: The Power of Visualization" from **Psychology Today**, research has revealed that mental practices are almost as effective as true physical practice.

- **MENTAL PRACTICES ENHANCE REAL-LIFE PERFORMANCE:** The article shows how mental practices, like visualization, can improve real-life performance in various fields, including sports and intellectual activities.
- **EVIDENCE FROM BRAIN STUDIES:** Brain studies have shown that imagining an activity activates the same brain patterns as physically doing it, showing the power of mental imagery in enhancing physical performance and skills.
- **APPLICATIONS IN SPORTS:** Many successful athletes, including Tiger Woods and Jack Nicklaus, use visualization techniques extensively to improve their performance, demonstrating its effectiveness in high-performance sports.
- **IMPACT ON MOTIVATION AND CONFIDENCE:** Visualization not only

improves physical skills but also boosts motivation, confidence, and self-efficacy, making it a powerful tool for personal development.

- TECHNIQUE FOR VISUALIZATION: The article suggests a method for effective visualization, which involves creating a detailed mental image of achieving a goal, engaging all senses, and practicing regularly to enhance performance and achieve personal goals.

Doing this with a partner/spouse is incredibly important, as it embeds an accountability partner and also provides space to dream. As years go by, you will see your dreams begin to converge and align, and you will realize you each have a unique part in helping the team achieve those dreams.

Here are five tips to get started:

- GATHER MATERIALS: Collect magazines, photos, quotes, and any other items that resonate with your goals.
- CHOOSE CATEGORIES: Organize your board into sections according to the categories of goals we discussed, such as finances, family, health, etc.
- BE SPECIFIC: Use images and words that precisely represent your specific goals, like a picture of a dream vacation spot for travel goals or a savings chart for financial goals.

- MAKE IT VISIBLE: Place your vision board somewhere you'll see it daily to keep your goals at the forefront of your mind.
- UPDATE REGULARLY: As you progress or your goals evolve, update your vision board to reflect these changes and maintain relevance.

Remember, making a vision board is a personal and creative process, so feel free to customize it in a way that best inspires and motivates you! We think putting an image to your goals not only makes things more fun; it also makes it more specific and more likely you will achieve that objective.

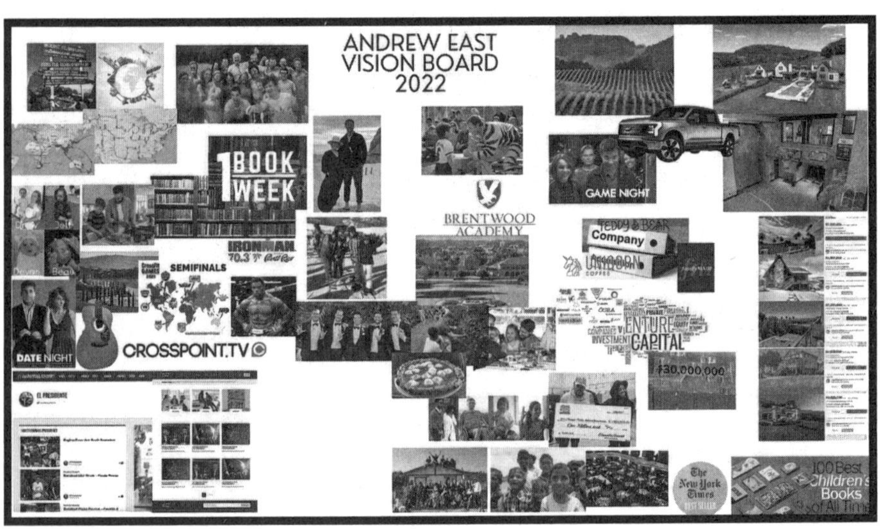
ANDREW EAST
VISION BOARD
2022
1 BOOK WEEK
IRONMAN 70.3
SEMIFINALS
DATE NIGHT
CROSSPOINT.TV
EL PRESIDENTE
BRENTWOOD ACADEMY
GAME NIGHT
TEDDY BEAR Company
VENTURE CAPITAL
$30,000,000
The New York Times BEST SELLER
100 Best Children's Books of All Time

EXAMPLE SESSION

2023 THEME: Prioritize family (ours and others) and making an impact. In deals we agree to, charities we give to, how we spend our time. Take care of Mom.

EXPAND ON: family mission statement, seasonal family traditions, and budget

Finances

- Income
  - ANDREW—$Y
  - SHAWN—$X
- Investments
  - Invest a total of $X
- Spending
  - Broadly—decrease personal spending, increase business investment spending (giveaways, advertising, website development, etc.)
  - Spend 3 percent of portfolio personally per the FIRE (Financial Independence, Retire Early) principle
- Charitable
  - ANDREW—account for $X of donations
  - SHAWN—account for $Y of donations

Travel
- ANDREW—Greek cruise, Disney
  - Travel budget $X
- SHAWN—Greek cruise, home Thanksgiving/Christmas

Family
- ANDREW—family, church 12x/year, Dad and kids another 12x/year (2x/month total), date night 36 times (3x/month), homemade lunch 3x/week, call Mom 3x/week, weekly family overview debrief
  - Seasonal family traditions—Valentine's Day outings as couple and with kids, Shawn's birthday, St. Patty's?, Easter, Memorial Day, 4th of July, Labor Day, Mom's birthday, pumpkin patch, apple orchard, Halloween, Thanksgiving, Christmas, New Year's
- SHAWN—quiet Sundays 35 weeks/year (church, no phones, activities, cooking, baking), 3x/week cooking at home, 2 dinners/month with Mimi and Papi, read books at bedtime every night, family walks 2x/week?

Friends
- ANDREW—men's group 24x/year, men's retreat, meal with a friend 1x/month
- SHAWN—game night 10x/year, send out 5 friends' thinking of you/checking in

texts a week, girls' night/book club 1x/
month, coffee 1x/month with a girlfriend,
Valentine's/birthday meals, one great
gift :)

Marriage

- ANDREW—date night 36 times (3x/month)
  alternating with surprises/adventures
- SHAWN—preplanned date nights (3x/
  month), alternating who plans devotionals
  3x/week

Health and Fitness

- ANDREW—get to 205 lbs., work out 5x/
  week, exercise with friend 1x/week
- SHAWN—get pregnant/healthy pregnancy

Philanthropy

- ANDREW—start a foundation, visit to
  children's hospital
- SHAWN—family missions trip

Home

- ANDREW—finish curtains, establish and
  agree on a clear monthly budget
- SHAWN—finish garage gym

Faith

- ANDREW—church 2x/month
- SHAWN—prayers before dinner, teach Drew
  Lord's Prayer

Business
- ANDREW—daylong work retreat
- SHAWN—start newsletter

Personal
- ANDREW—focus on transparency and grace with truth with Shawn and close friends, FINALLY get my pilot's license
- SHAWN—two tattoos, vision board

Kids
- ANDREW—create/write down seasonal traditions, finish playroom w/climbing and pit
- SHAWN—Jett saying 100 words, Drew finish potty training and transition into big girl bed

TEMPLATE

Finances
- EXPLANATION: Addressing financial health and stability, including income, spending, investments, and charitable donations.
- EXAMPLE GOALS:
  - Increase savings by 10 percent.
  - Reduce personal spending by 15 percent.

- Invest a set amount in a diversified portfolio.
- Allocate a specific percentage of income to charitable causes.

Travel
- EXPLANATION: Planning trips and vacations to enhance family bonds and create memorable experiences.
- EXAMPLE GOALS:
  - Plan a family vacation to Greece.
  - Set a travel budget and stick to it.
  - Visit a new country or state.
  - Organize a camping trip with extended family.

Family
- EXPLANATION: Strengthening family relationships through shared activities and traditions.
- EXAMPLE GOALS:
  - Establish new family traditions like a yearly pumpkin patch visit.
  - Commit to family dinners 2x/week.
  - Plan monthly family outings.
  - Create a family mission statement.

Friends
- EXPLANATION: Nurturing friendships and building a supportive community.

- EXAMPLE GOALS:
  - Host a monthly game night.
  - Attend or organize a men's/women's retreat.
  - Send weekly "thinking of you" messages to friends.
  - Establish a book club or regular coffee meetups.

Marriage

- EXPLANATION: Focusing on the marital relationship, ensuring ongoing growth and connection.
- EXAMPLE GOALS:
  - Plan regular date nights, alternating who organizes them.
  - Start a weekly devotion or meditation practice together.
  - Attend a couples' retreat or workshop.
  - Commit to a monthly relationship check-in.

Health and Fitness

- EXPLANATION: Setting goals for physical health, fitness, and overall well-being.
- EXAMPLE GOALS:
  - Reach a target weight or fitness level.
  - Establish a consistent workout routine.
  - Train for and complete a half-marathon.
  - Incorporate a balanced diet into daily life.

Philanthropy
- EXPLANATION: Contributing to society through charitable acts and volunteerism.
- EXAMPLE GOALS:
  - Start a family foundation or fund.
  - Volunteer at a local charity or community event.
  - Organize a charity fundraiser.
  - Make regular visits to a children's hospital.

Home
- EXPLANATION: Creating a comfortable, functional, and joyful living space.
- EXAMPLE GOALS:
  - Complete home improvement projects like curtain installation.
  - Establish a clear monthly budget for home expenses.
  - Design and set up a home gym or play area.
  - Organize and declutter the living space.

Faith
- EXPLANATION: Cultivating spiritual growth and practices within the family.
- EXAMPLE GOALS:
  - Attend church or spiritual services regularly.
  - Implement daily or weekly prayer sessions.
  - Teach children about spiritual values and practices.

- Participate in a faith-based community event.

Business

- EXPLANATION: Advancing career or business aspirations through strategic goals.
- EXAMPLE GOALS:
  - Organize a strategic planning retreat for the business.
  - Launch a new product or service.
  - Expand the business network through industry events.
  - Start a business newsletter or blog.

Personal

- EXPLANATION: Personal development goals focusing on self-improvement and hobbies.
- EXAMPLE GOALS:
  - Learn a new skill or hobby, like piloting or painting.
  - Read a book a month for personal growth.
  - Attend a workshop or course for personal development.
  - Practice daily mindfulness or meditation.

Kids

- EXPLANATION: Focusing on the growth, education, and happiness of children.
- EXAMPLE GOALS:
  - Establish educational routines like reading before bed.

- Plan and execute seasonal family activities.
- Set developmental milestones for each child.
- Encourage a new hobby or sport for the kids.

These sections and example goals provide a comprehensive framework for family goal setting, covering all aspects of life from personal to professional, ensuring a balanced approach to growth and fulfillment.

NOTES

CHAPTER 1: CALM

8   In 2011, researchers published a groundbreaking: Shai Danziger, Jonathan Levav, and Liora Avnaim-Pesso, "Extraneous Factors in Judicial Decisions," **Proceedings of the National Academy of Science** 108, no. 17 (April 2011): 6889–92, doi.org/10.1073/pnas.1018033108.

9   "Because I have too many other decisions": **Vanity Fair**, "Barack Obama to Michael Lewis on a Presidential Loss of Freedom: 'You Don't Get Used to It—At Least, I Don't,'" **Vanity Fair**, September 5, 2012, vanityfair.com/news/2012/09/barack-obama-michael-lewis.

13 In experiments at the University: Thomas L. Saltsman, Mark D. Seery, Cheryl L. Kondrak, Veronica M. Lamarche, and Lindsey Streamer, "Too Many Fish in the Sea: A Motivational Examination of the Choice Overload Experience," **Biological Psychology** 145 (July 2019): 17–30, doi.org/10.1016/j.biopsycho.2019.03.010.

CHAPTER 2: JOY

21 Studies have found that couples: Michelle Roth, Selina A. Landolt, Fridtjof W. Nussbeck, Katharina Weitkamp, and Guy Bodenmann, "Positive Outcomes of Long-Term Relationship Satisfaction Trajectories in Stable Romantic Couples: A 10-Year Longitudinal Study," **International Journal of Applied Positive Psychology** 10, no. 8 (December 2024), link.springer.com/article/10.1007/s41042 -024-00201-1; Ali Rogin and Claire Mufson, "Researchers Find Strong Relationships Protect Long-Term Health and Happiness," PBS, November 26, 2023, pbs.org /newshour/show/researchers-find-strong-relationships -protect-long-term-health-and-happiness.

23 Researchers studying this group: Todd B. Kashdan and Patrick E. McKnight, "Commitment to a Purpose in Life: An Antidote to the Suffering by Individuals with Social Anxiety Disorder," **Emotion** 13, no. 6 (December 2013): 1150–59, pubmed.ncbi.nlm.nih.gov/23795592.

27 When presented with a limited array: Sheena S. Iyengar and Mark R. Lepper, "When Choice Is Demotivating: Can One Desire Too Much of a Good Thing?" **Journal of Personality and Social Psychology** 79, no. 6 (December 2000): 995–1006, doi.org/10.1037/0022-3514.79.6.995.

27–28 Studies in positive psychology: Iyengar and Lepper, "When Choice Is Demotivating."

28 Musicians who practice with focus: John Kounios and David S. Rosen, "Brain Scans of Jazz Musicians Reveal How to Reach a Creative 'Flow State,'" **Scientific American**, May 30, 2024, scientificamerican.com/article/brain-scans-of -jazz-musicians-reveal-how-to-reach-a-creative-flow-state; Drexel University, "New Study Reveals How the Brain Achieves a Flow State," **SciTechDaily**, March 17, 2024,

scitechdaily.com/new-study-reveals-how-the-brain -achieves-a-flow-state.

CHAPTER 3: DEPTH

35 Anders Ericsson's landmark research: K. Anders Ericsson, Ralf T. Krampe, and Clemens Tesch-Romer, "The Role of Deliberate Practice in the Acquisition of Expert Performance," **Psychological Review** 100, no. 3 (1993): 363–406, graphics8.nytimes.com/images/blogs/freako nomics/pdf/DeliberatePractice(PsychologicalReview) .pdf.

35 A fascinating 2025 study: Morgan Williams, Marek Palace, James Welsh, and Samantha Brooks, "Neural Correlates of Chess Expertise: A Systematic Review of Brain Imaging Studies Comparing Expert Versus Novice Players," **Brain Mechanisms** 148–50 (October–December 2025), doi.org/10.1016/j.bramec.2025.202516.

40 A fascinating body of research: Sarah Benz, Roberta Sellaro, Bernhard Hommel, and Lorenza S. Colzato "Music Makes the World Go Round: The Impact of Muscial Training on Non-Musical Cognitive Functions—A Review," **Frontiers in Psychology** 6 (January 2016), doi .org/10.3389/fpsyg.2015.02023; Ewa A. Miendlarzewska and Wiebke J. Trost, "How Musical Training Affects Cognitive Development: Rhythm, Reward and Other Modulating Variables," **Frontiers in Neuroscience** 7 (January 2014): 279, doi.org/10.3389/fnins .2013.00279.

CHAPTER 5: MEANING

70 This is what behavioral economists: Michael I. Norton, Daniel Mochon, and Dan Ariely, "The 'IKEA Effect':

When Labor Leads to Love," Working Paper No. 11-091, Harvard Business School, 2011, hbs.edu/ris/Publication %20Files/11-091.pdf.

75 Consider a curious finding: Hal R. Arkes, Cynthia A. Joyner, Mark V. Pezzo, Jane Gradwohl Nash, Karen Siegel-Jacobs, and Eric Stone, "The Psychology of Windfall Gains," **Organizational Behavior and Human Decision Processes** 59, no. 3 (September 1994): 331–47, doi.org/10.1006/obhd.1994.1063; Hal Hershfield, "The Psychology of Financial Windfalls: How Unexpected Money Influences Spending Behavior," Avantis Investors, June 30, 2025, avantisinvestors.com /avantis-insights/psychology-financial-windfalls.

76 This mirrors what psychologists call: Michael Inzlicht, Amitai Shenhav, and Christopher Y. Olivola, "The Effort Paradox: Effort Is Both Costly and Valued," **Trends in Cognitive Sciences** 22, no. 4 (April 2018): 337–49, doi .org/10.1016/j.tics.2018.01.007; Aidan V. Campbell, Yiyi Wang, and Michael Inzlicht, "Experimental Evidence That Exerting Effort Increases Meaning," **Cognition** 257 (April 2025), doi.org/10.1016/j.cognition.2025 .106065.

77 The same pattern appears: Elizabeth Bjork and Robert Bjork, "Making Things Hard on Yourself, but in a Good Way: Creating Desirable Difficulties to Enhance Learning," in **Psychology and the Real World: Essays Illustrating Fundamental Contributions to Society**, ed. Morton Ann Gernsbacher (Worth Publishers, 2011), 55–64, researchgate.net/publication/284097727_Making _things_hard_on_yourself_but_in_a_good_way_ Creating_desirable_difficulties_to_enhance_learning.

CHAPTER 11: BOREDOM

182 A 2021 study from USC: Psychologist Wendy Wood's research at USC demonstrates that habits and goals operate through separate brain systems. Once formed, habits are triggered automatically by context cues—which may explain why showing up gets easier over time. See Wendy Wood, Asaf Mazar, and David T. Neal, "Habits and Goals in Human Behavior: Separate but Interacting Systems," **Perspectives on Psychological Science** 16, no. 4 (2021): 1–16.

184 A study on perceived control: Andriy A. Struk, Abigail A. Scholer, and James Danckert, "Perceptions of Control Influence Feelings of Boredom," **Frontiers in Psychology** 12 (July 2021), doi.org/10.3389 /fpsyg.2021.687623.

CHAPTER 13: ENVIRONMENT

214 Researchers have found that cluttered: Boyoun (Grace) Chae and Rui (Juliet) Zhu, "Why a Messy Workspace Undermines Your Persistence," **Harvard Business Review**, January 22, 2015, hbr.org/2015/01/why -a-messy-workspace-undermines-your-persistence.

215 Research shows that about 43 percent: Chris Palmer, "Harnessing the Power of Habits: The Habit Lab at the University of Southern California Explores How We Form Habits and How We Can Change Unwanted Ones," **Monitor on Psychology** 51, no. 8 (November/December 2020): 78, apa.org/monitor/2020/11/career-lab-habits; Wendy Wood, Jeffrey M. Quinn, and Deborah A. Kashy, "Habits in Everyday Life: Thought, Emotion, and Action," **Journal of Personality and Social Psychology** 83, no. 6 (2002): 1281–97, doi.org/10.1037/0022-3514.83.6.1281.

CHAPTER 15: METRICS

247 Dr. Albert Bandura's landmark research: Jessica A. Chen, Eliot Fearey, and Ronald E. Smith, "'That Which Is Measured Improves': A Theoretical and Empirical Review of Self-Monitoring in Self-Management and Adaptive Behavior Change," **Journal of Behavior Therapy and Mental Health** 1, no. 4 (May 2017): 19–38, doi.org/10.14302/issn.2474-9273.jbtm-16-1180.

248 Studies of habit formation show: Ben Singh, Andrew Murphy, Carol Maher, and Ashleigh E Smith, "Time to Form a Habit: A Systematic Review and Meta-Analysis of Health Behaviour Habit Formation and Its Determinants," **Healthcare** 12, no. 23 (December 2024): 2488, doi.org/10.3390/healthcare12232488.

CHAPTER 16: BELIEF

267 In 2004, exercise physiologist: Vinoth K. Ranganathan, Vlodek Siemionow, Jing Z. Liu, Vinod Sahgal, and Guang H. Yue, "From Mental Power to Muscle Power—Gaining Strength by Using Mind," **Neuropsychologia** 42, no. 7 (2004): 944–56, doi.org/10.1016/j.neuropsychologia.2003.11.0.

267 His research team recruited: Ellen Goodman, "Mind Over Muscle," **Washington Post**, January 11, 2002, washingtonpost.com/archive/opinions/2002/01/12/mind-over-muscle/12a0daa7-d8f6-43ed-934f-c5163602c26c.

CHAPTER 17: COSTS

283 Back in 1985, psychologists: Hal Richard Arkes and Catherine Blumer, "The Psychology of Sunk Cost,"

Organizational Behavior and Human Decision Processes 35, no. 1 (February 1985): 124–40, doi.org/10.1016/0749-5978(85)90049-4.

284 They sold season tickets: Arkes and Blumer, "The Psychology of Sunk Cost."

CHAPTER 18: GRACE

302 In one particularly telling study: Kristen D. Neff, "Self-Compassion: Theory, Method, Research, and Intervention," **Annual Review of Psychology** 74 (January 2023): 193–218, doi.org/10.1146/annurev-psych-032420-031047.

303 Juliana Breines and Serena Chen at UC Berkeley: Juliana G. Breines and Serena Chen, "Self-Compassion Increases Self-Improvement Motivation," **Personality and Social Psychology Bulletin** 38, no. 9 (September 2012): 1133–43, doi.org/10.1177/0146167212445599.

APPENDIX: THE EAST FAMILY VISION SETTING METHOD

337 research has revealed that mental practices: Angie LeVan, "Seeing Is Believing: The Power of Visualization," **Psychology Today**, December 3, 2009, psychologytoday.com/us/blog/flourish/200912/seeing-is-believing-the-power-visualization; citing Vinoth K. Ranganathan, Vlodek Siemionow, Jing Z. Liu, Vinod Sahgal, and Guang H. Yue, "From Mental Power to Muscle Power—Gaining Strength by Using the Mind," **Neuropsychologia** 42, no. 7 (2004): 944–56, doi.org/10.1016/j.neuropsychologia.2003.11.0.

ABOUT THE AUTHORS

SHAWN JOHNSON is a former gymnast; a three-time US all-around champion in women's gymnastics; and the 2008 Olympic balance beam gold medalist and team, all-around, and floor exercise silver medalist. She is also the winner of season eight of **Dancing with the Stars**.

ANDREW EAST is a former NFL long snapper and played college football at Vanderbilt. Shawn and Andrew met in 2012, married in 2016, and now live in Tennessee with their three children.